"By far the best short guide to Arab, cultures . . . an invaluable resource."
—Jack Shaheen, *Reel Bad Arabs*

"Too often people learn from experiences that do not represent the larger truth. Nawar's book—and his life's work—focuses on the type of understanding, compassion, and insight that transforms people, interactions, and outcomes. A must-read for any leader representing, policing, or interacting with people of Arab descent... so, all of us."
—Kristina Tanasichuk, Executive Editor, Homeland Security Today;
President, Women in Homeland Security

"This book is a critical and bold guide that will deepen readers' understandings of the Arab and Muslim communities in the United States. At times personal, at times probing, Nawar pulls no punches as he confronts the stereotypes and misinformation that drive ignorance and hate against these communities.
—Brie Loskota, Executive Director, Center for the Public
Understanding of Religion, University of Chicago

"As someone deeply involved in interfaith dialogue and the US/Israel relationship, I quickly became aware of how uninformed and ignorant I was of both the Muslim faith and the Arab-American experience. *Muslims, Arabs, and Arab-Americans* became my invaluable guide to better understand my Muslim brothers and sisters and highlight the lack of understanding and nuance in my own world view. Thanks to this book, I have grown to become a strong advocate for Muslim Americans fighting Islamophobia and prejudice and now proudly stand shoulder to shoulder with Arab-Americans on many issues. A good book makes you smarter; a great book makes you a better person. I believe *Muslims, Arabs, and Arab-Americans* has helped me become both and I am very grateful."
—Rabbi Victor Urecki, Congregation B'nai Jacob, Charleston, West
Virginia

For my grandparents . . .

And my grandchildren.

**Nawar Shora**

# MUSLIMS, ARABS & ARAB AMERICANS

Cune

*Muslims, Arabs and Arab Americans:*
*A Quick Guide to Islamic and Arabic Culture*
© 2024 Nawar Shora
Cune Press, Seattle 2024

Library of Congress Cataloging-in-Publication Data

Names: Shora, Nawar, author.
Title: Muslims, Arabs & Arab-Americans : a quick guide to Islamic and
  Arabic culture / by Nawar Shora.
Other titles: Arab-American handbook | Muslims, Arabs and Arab-Americans
Description: Third edition. | Seattle : Cune, 2024. | Includes
  bibliographical references.
Identifiers: LCCN 2023047307 (print) | LCCN 2023047308 (ebook) | ISBN
  9781951082406 (trade paperback) | ISBN 9781614574347 (epub)
Subjects: LCSH: Arab Americans--Handbooks, manuals, etc. |
  Arabs--Handbooks, manuals, etc. | Muslims--Handbooks, manuals, etc.
Classification: LCC E184.A65 S56 2024  (print) | LCC E184.A65  (ebook) |
  DDC 305.892/7073--dc23/eng/20240108
LC record available at https://lccn.loc.gov/2023047307
LC ebook record available at https://lccn.loc.gov/2023047308

Calligraphy by Mamoun Sakkal (www.sakkaldesign.com). Illustrations by Ali Farzat (www.alifarzat.com). At a Glance by Andrea Stanton. Thanks to Steven Schlesser for his historical and editorial support.

Thanks to the Salaam Cultural Museum for its encouragement and support.

Bridge Between the Cultures (a series from Cune Press)

| | |
|---|---|
| The Passionate Spies | John Harte |
| Music Has No Boundaries | Rafiq Gangat |
| Jinwar and Other Stories | Alex Poppe |
| Kivu: Travels in Eastern Congo | Frederic Hunter |
| Empower a Refuge | Patricia Martin Holt |
| White Carnations | Musa Rahum Abbas |
| Afghanistan & Beyond | Linda Sartor |
| Girl Fighters | Carolyn Han |
| Apartheid Is a Crime | Mats Svensson |
| Curse of the Achille Lauro | Reem al-Nimer |
| The Dusk Visitor | Musa Al-Halool |
| Old Enough to Know | Alice Rothchild |
| Escape to Aswan | Amal Sedky Winter |

Cune  Cune Press: www.cunepress.com

As members of the one human family and as believers, we have obligations to the common good, to justice and to solidarity.

—Pope John Paul II
The Umayyad Mosque
Damascus, May 2001

# Contents

# Introduction

"WE HAVE THE OPPORTUNITY TO IMMIGRATE TO AMERICA"—I remember my parents sitting my brother and I down while we were residing in Jeddah, Saudi Arabia to share the good news. I remember being excited at the chance. In my head, I was recalling Disney World and the Smithsonian Museums, but the reality was initially far different in Huntington, West Virginia. It was 1987, and the first few years were very tough on this short, fat, hairy, Arab, Muslim kid who suffered from Scrappy syndrome and didn't back down from a fight. I won some, I lost some... I even got knocked out by a junior golden glove boxer. There was fear and misunderstanding and even hatred towards me, to say the least. I resisted caving into the brewing resentment and give into reciprocating the hate.

Despite the difficulty, good people exist—as Mr Rogers taught us, "look for the helpers" - within a few years, I made some genuine friends, I learned to follow American Football, and at the beginning of Gulf War 1, I built up enough confidence and ran for Freshman class president... and lost miserably. As part of the nomination process, I needed peer signatures, sadly, a number wrote down aliases like "Osama Bin Laden" or "Saddam Hussein". Still, the passion had taken hold and I was shedding my label of the guy with the weird name or "seed sandwich" lunch, let alone the "Camel jockey" or "Terrorist" and was redefining who I am. I ran again for tenth grade president (my campaign speech was a poem) and this time, somehow, I won! A year later, I was elected the first Junior to serve as Student Body President in the 100-year history of my high school. I was no longer just accepted; I was supported with amazing friends and classmates. It wasn't that I lost my ethnicity or faith, it's that I was able to go beyond them and melt them into my overall "American-ness". My mother had ingrained in me the balance between my Arab, Muslim, and American cultures.

In 1994, I entered college with two goals: Serve as Student Body President and graduate within three years. Two years in, I was elected president and graduated the third year, and twenty-four years later, in 2018, I returned to my Alma Mater as the Commencement Speaker. To this day, one of the greatest moments of my life, to stand there before thousands of graduates and their families and share my inner thoughts on dreams, success, greatness and especially failure. Themes included going beyond conquering your dreams, rather conquering your reality! I reminded every single one of the graduates how "Mark Zuckerberg is not better than you" and to go out to change the world for the better.

After a tough first year in law school—I hear Micky from Rocky saying "I didn't hear no bell!" - I graduated law school in 2001, and priorities instantly changed in the aftermath of 9/11, and I went to protect civil rights and forge relationships with law enforcement and government entities at a time when some people thought me crazy to meet, even train, police and the FBI. Success bred success and in 2009 I received the FBI Director's Community Leadership Award and in 2011 the story came full circle with the DHS American By Choice Award. I am a proud American by choice, my son is a proud American while embracing fully his Arab and French sides and we are all better for it. In a time of continued fear, mistrust, and uncertainty, I am proud of my immigrant story, and I will always be proud to be an American.

The aim of this book is to help demystify. I've said for years our greatest enemy in society is the lack of trust. We get to lack of trust through lack of communication and lack of understanding. If we flip all those elements into the positive, the formula is simple:

Communication + Understanding = Trust

If we truly know how to effectively communicate, if we fully understand one another, then the genuine, authentic trust will bloom organically. This book and its simple lessons aim to demystify the Muslim and Arab communities and people, in addition to those often confused for being so, such as Persians or Sikhs. This book is ultimately about building trust, building relationships, and connecting with others. I hope you will find it helpful, as it is based on my time-tested seminars that I have been fortunate enough to give across the country and the world for over two decades.

I am thankful my parents had the opportunity to move to the United States, and I am grateful for the journey. We continue our growth, we continue our struggle, and we continue our gratitude! May we, as a nation, forever remain what President Reagan called "the Shining City on a Hill."

# Section One

An easy-to-read, test-your-knowledge quiz that challenges misperceptions about Muslims, Arabs and Arab-Americans. This is followed by detailed answers and explanations.

# Contents (Section One)

## For Your Information

## Points to Ponder

**Illustrations**

# A Note to the Reader

THIS BOOK AIMS TO INFORM YOU ABOUT MUSLIMS, ARABS and Arab-Americans. It is designed for everyone in society, from civil servants (in the military, law enforcement, border patrol, or homeland security), to academia and corporations, as well as the general public. The book provides objective and honest, general, apolitical information: cultures, demographics, history, languages, and religions.

You may choose to read the book in its entirety, or instead use it as a reference book and skip between the sections of greatest interest to you. *Muslims, Arabs and Arab-Americans* is so named because Muslims, Arabs and Arab-Americans are often lumped together by a public that assumes they are all adherents of Islam. Distinctions among these groups will be made throughout the book. Please note that statistics provided in this edition are up-to-date as of August 2022.

It's my hope that readers will walk away with a newfound understanding and appreciation of Muslims, Arabs, and Arab-Americans—the people, the cultures, the languages, the habits. Most important: I hope to demystify these groups and to lower the level of fear, mistrust, and apprehension as I have been doing for over two decades through my seminars and lectures.

Nawar Shora, JD
Washington, DC

# Introductory Quiz

THIS BOOK IS GUIDED BY A BASIC FORMULA THAT summarizes the root of the many challenges we face as a society:

Lack of Understanding + Lack of Communication = Lack of Trust

Trust is the key factor to unlock a clearer future for all of us. Once we secure trust between the public, the government and those minority communities most affected by 9/11 (including Arabs, Arab-Americans, Sikhs, South Asians, Iranians, Turks, and Muslims as a religious group), we can achieve a great deal together, making valuable progress towards genuine trust. The more accurate—and more positive—illustration of the above formula is:

Understanding + Communication = Trust

If I understand you, if we learn how to communicate, then the trust will organically grow. It applies to these communities, it applies across society. This book will target the first element of *understanding*. Often, distrust of others comes from the fact that we believe them to be different from ourselves. Chief Joseph of the Wallowa Native Americans said: "We fear that which we do not understand." The less mainstream Americans know about Arabs and Muslims, the greater the likelihood of hostility between them.

I have been doing diversity-awareness training with governments, church groups, corporations, universities, law enforcement and others for over two decades and have reached thousands upon thousands of individuals in that time. Often the best way to start is to catch people off guard, to quiz them on how much they actually know about a subject. That is what I tend to do in my presentations. My quiz is never graded, however, and the answers remain anonymous. It is intended to be used as a teaching tool and a vehicle for discussion.

So let's take the quiz!

It's made up of ten straightforward questions. If you are unsure of your answers, mark something down, even if it's only a guess. If you feel completely stumped, check with a friend, a colleague, or a family member—this won't be considered cheating. As each of the answers will be explained to you later, there is no need to do any research to seek out the right answers.

Take fifteen minutes on average to complete the quiz—though you may take more time if you need. Remember that questions six and seven ask you to name a character, and not an actor and I'm looking for the ethnicity, not the religion. In question ten, there is at least one Arab-American in each category. Now go ahead and start. Good luck!

1. On a scale from one to ten, with one being least and ten being most, how much do you know about Muslims, Arabs and Arab-Americans?

2. True or False: All Arabs are Muslim, and all Muslims are Arab.

3. What is the world's most populous Muslim country?

4. What is the first thing that comes to mind when you hear the term 'Muslim' or 'Arab'?

5. True or False: Muslims or Arab-Americans were responsible for the Oklahoma City bombing.

6. Name one or more positive Arab *characters* in television history.

7. Name one or more positive Arab *characters* in movie history.

8. True or False: Arab-Americans were responsible for the 9/11 attacks on the US.

9. Do you believe a negative stereotype exists of Muslims or Arab-Americans in the United States?

10. Circle the Arab-American public figure(s) in each of the following categories:

| | | |
|---|---|---|
| A. Shakira | Christina Aguilera | Britney Spears |
| B. Ralph Nader | Al Gore | Mitt Romney |
| C. Salma Hayek | Shannon Elizabeth | Denise Richards |
| D. Debbie Gibson | Paula Abdul | Tiffany |

E. Doug Flutie            Jeff George            Drew Brees

F. Shaggy                 Fred Flintstone        Homer Simpson

In the next sections, you will learn the correct answers to the quiz, and will discover the most common questions and comments I receive after administering the quiz in my own presentations.

# Chapter One

# Muslims & Arabs

## A Discussion of the Introductory Quiz

THIS FIRST CHAPTER OF THE BOOK USES the answers to the Introductory Quiz as a framework for presenting some basic information about Arabs and Muslims.

Topics to be discussed:

- Basic knowledge about Muslims, Arabs and Arab-Americans.
- Immigrant behavior and mannerisms.
- Perceptions of Muslims, Arabs and Arab-Americans.
- Domestic and international population statistics on Arabs and Muslims.
- What makes a country an Arab country?

Points to Remember:

- Arabs are a multiracial, religiously diverse, heterogeneous group of people.
- Arab is the ethnicity.
- Muslims believe they are followers of the third and final Abrahamic faith, continuing from Judaism and Christianity.
- Muslims live all over the world, although their largest populations are in South and Southeast Asia.
- Arabs live in what is commonly referred to as the Middle East (though Southwest Asia is technically more correct) and North Africa (MENA).
- Learn the Three Factor Test to determine an Arab country:
  - A cultural and historical link;

- One majority religion, Islam, although not always the only one practiced;
- One majority language, Arabic, with many different dialects, although not always the only language spoken.

## Question One

### On a scale from one to ten how much do you know about Muslims, Arabs, and Arab-Americans?

Of the thousands of individuals who have taken the quiz, most respondents rank themselves as one, two or three. Some label themselves four, five or six. Few assign themselves eight or more, including people who are familiar with Arabs and Muslims.

Indeed, the majority of individuals who have taken this quiz believe that they know little about Muslims, Arabs, Arab-Americans, or Arab culture. Such honest self-appraisal is good news, although it would be preferable if all quiz takers knew enough to give themselves a top grade! However, it's far better to recognize one's lack of knowledge, than to believe that one knows more than one actually does. Ignorance or lack of knowledge is regrettable, but not dangerous. The false perception of knowledge, on the other hand, is dangerous.

Here is an example. In an informal survey conducted in a university setting, 25% of those who graded themselves seven or higher, believed that Muslims or Arab-Americans were involved in the Oklahoma City bombing—a bombing that killed 168 people, many of whom were children—on April 19, 1995. This, of course, is plain wrong. It was heartland Americans—Tim McVeigh and Terry Nichols—who committed this crime. Such false knowledge plants seeds of misunderstanding, bigotry, and hatred. We will address this problem in more detail, when discussing questions six and seven about media portrayals.

Why respondents believe they know so little:

Many quiz respondents realize they don't know much about this topic. Here are the reasons they give for their lack of knowledge:

- We don't learn about these people in school.
- We aren't sure why we should learn about them.

- We don't know about them because they don't play a significant role in our society.

- We don't know about them because they don't know about us.

- We don't know about them because they choose to stay away from the rest of us.

- We don't know about them because the media taught us everything we know.

Let's address some of these explanations.

*We do not learn about Muslims, Arabs, or Arab-Americans, in school.*

This is true for two reasons. First, most of the history and culture we learn about in school is rooted in Judeo-Christian and Anglo-European traditions. A study by the Center for Middle Eastern and North African Studies of eighty textbooks showed that materials about Arabs and Muslims in them tended to rely on stereotypes, based on overly simplistic or inaccurate information. In addition, textbooks rarely presented facts and/or perceptions from the perspective of Arabs and/or Muslims themselves.[2] As a result, a large group of immigrants, whose cultures have helped shape American society, are thus ignored and denigrated. Arabs and Muslims have been part of America even before the United States became a nation. They played a significant role in shaping world history, and in positively influencing American society.

The second reason is this: generally, the US educational system tends to ignore the rest of the world. Most students learn little world geography, investigate few societies other than their own, and study few foreign languages. Several National Geographic Society surveys confirmed this state of affairs. They showed that American men and women, aged eighteen to twenty-four, knew little about either world or domestic geography (these studies will be discussed later).

When I was in high school, my fellow students and I rarely had to consult a world map. Our course work hardly ever scratched the surface of the world beyond our own shores. While many of our institutions of higher learning have excellent departments of Middle Eastern and Islamic studies, their curricula are not integrated into other departments. Unless students make a determined effort to learn about Arabs—the people, their history and culture, or to study Muslims—their faith and their diversity as a community, they literally "will not learn about them in school." One would think world civilization started in England in the seventeenth century!

*We aren't sure why we should learn about them.*

Many respondents wonder, almost defensively, why such an understanding is necessary or useful.

Here's why. First, given the terrorist activities the United States and its allies now face, we as a society (including those in all areas of government, especially law enforcement or security careers) need to learn to accurately understand Muslims, Arabs, and Arab-Americans, and not on the basis of the false perceptions mentioned earlier, but to differentiate between a faith, an ethnicity, and a violent ideology. For example, understanding something about Islam will help us discern how violent extremists manipulate and misinterpret it when seeking to justify terrorism.

Secondly, understanding what Islam is will help thwart false perceptions, and end the intolerance and hatred bred by fear, and spread on both sides in the name of religion.

A third reason is that knowledge about Arabs and Muslims will curb the targeting of innocent people, based solely on dress, appearance, preconceptions, or stereotypes.

What will happen if we gain a better understanding of Arab and Muslim communities, both here and abroad? Tensions will be reduced. We will come to realize that these people have the same goals as do most Americans. They want peace, prosperity, and better lives for their children. Such understanding would make it possible not only to make Americans feel safer, but to literally work together for a better world.

*We don't know about them because they don't play a significant role in our society.*

In fact, Arabs and Muslims have played important roles throughout US history. They continue to do so today. Many Americans are unfamiliar with the range of societal roles played by Arab-Americans and American Muslims. Among those of Arab descent are Ralph Nader; White House press corps legend Helen Thomas; General John Abizaid, former commander of the United States Central Command; and acclaimed actor and multiple Emmy award winner, Tony Shalhoub. American Muslims include revolutionary doctor Ayub Ommaya, famous entertainers Ice Cube and Dave Chappelle, poet Pamela K. Taylor, and legendary athletes, Shaq, Mike Tyson, Kareem Abdul Jabbar and Muhammed Ali. This question will be addressed more fully when we discuss question ten about significant Arab and Muslim figures in American society.

*We don't know about them because they don't know about us.*

Millions of Muslims and Arabs do know about us because they are *us*! Most Arabs in this country are Arab-Americans. Of the three to four million of them, about 83.3% are United States citizens. 46% were born here. Over half of foreign-born Arabs are naturalized citizens.[3] A sizable percentage of the 16.7% of non-citizen Arabs come here to study at universities throughout the United States.[4] Others come on business, as tourists or to visit relatives.

Many Arabs and Muslims living elsewhere are very familiar with the United States and Americans, and with many aspects of American popular culture. They watch our movies. They listen to our music. Moreover, for decades, American foreign policy has played an important role in Arab politics, most acutely since 9/11, and the war on Iraq in 2003.

This book mentioned "false perceptions." Our music and movies may tend to present false impressions of American life as being violent, sex-obsessed, and characterized by too much chaos and too little discipline. As a result, Muslims or Arabs who suppose that armed criminals hang out on every American street-corner or that most American teenage girls are single mothers, are sadly ill-informed. They are like those Americans who see the world in terms of "us" and "them," who suppose that "we" are light-skinned and democratic and Christian, whereas "they" are dark-skinned and extremist and Muslim.

If some Mulsims or Arabs have false perceptions about America, many others, especially the elites, follow US politics very closely, by reading and watching our news media via the internet or satellite television. They sometimes know about us more than we know about ourselves, and for three main reasons:

Firstly, US culture reaches across borders. Its delivery systems are dominant. So is its language. English is increasingly taught in schools all over the world.

Secondly, individuals outside the United States study the cultures and languages of other peoples, because they believe that such study enhances their world awareness and their prosperity. For example, only 23% of Americans speak a language other than English. By contrast, in eighty-five countries where English is not the native tongue, it is the premiere influential second language of trade, tourism, and hip youth culture. This is the case in Arab countries such as Egypt and Jordan, and in Muslim countries such as Pakistan and Malaysia.

Thirdly, like many people around the globe, Arabs and Muslims understand the need to learn about different countries and cultures, because these provide insights into other nations' political and economic policies. Because of globalization, cultures are becoming more intertwined. Present US dominance in cultural globalization, politics and economics requires others to learn about it.

## Question Two

### True or False: All Arabs are Muslim . . . and all Muslims are Arab.

False! Because the terms "Arab" and "Muslim" are often used interchangeably in conversation and sometimes in media reports, many people now believe that the two groups are one and the same. However, not all Arabs are Muslims, nor are all Muslims Arabs. Let's analyze the distinctions.

### Who are the Arabs and what makes an Arab country?

Arabs are a multiracial, religiously diverse, heterogeneous group of approximately three hundred million people living in, or originating from, Southwest Asia and North Africa.

> FYI – Terminology: Middle East
> *We should note that the Arab World and the Middle East are not the same. Geographically speaking, the Arab World lies in Southwest Asia and North Africa. "Middle East" is a term coined by the British, to distinguish what was, for them, an area between the "Far East" and the "Near East." The Middle East includes non-Arab countries such as Turkey, Israel, and Iran. A more inclusive term is Middle East North African or MENA Americans.*

The Arab World is generally considered to include the members of the League of Arab States (the Arab League). There are twenty-two countries in the Arab League reaching across North Africa into parts of the Middle East. They are: Algeria, Bahrain, the Comoros Islands, Djibouti, Egypt, Iraq, Jordan, Kuwait, Lebanon, Libya, Mauritania, Morocco, Oman, Palestine, Qatar, Saudi Arabia, Somalia, Sudan, Syria, Tunisia, the United Arab Emirates, and Yemen. Although Sudan is considered an Arab country, its population in the north is mainly Arab, while that of the south is comprised mainly of non-Arabic speakers. Other countries in the region have large percentages of Arabs and native Arabic speakers but are not generally considered to be Arab countries. South Sudan – predominantly, non-Arab or Muslim, became its own country in 2011.

The majority of Arabs live in the continent of Africa. A woman from Morocco might describe herself as a Moroccan, as an Arab (if she is not Berber or another ethnic minority), and as an African. All three descriptions are apt, and all are true at the same time.

So what exactly makes an Arab country? Why is Tunisia an Arab country, but not Iran? Why is Syria an Arab country, while its neighbor Turkey is not? Why is Bahrain an Arab country, but not Israel? The answer cannot solely be geographical, because Arab and non-Arab countries are found in the same region. Iran and Turkey are the two countries most often confused for being Arab.

Let's look at an analogy more familiar to Americans. The Arab World is linked together—in much the same way as Latin America is—through three dominant factors: (1) a cultural/historical link; (2) a majority religion, though not the only one practiced; and (3) a majority language, often with many different dialects, although not the only one spoken. Each factor helps to distinguish countries as Arab. A country is not Arab unless all three factors are present.

> FYI—Morocco
> *In 1777, Morocco became the first country to recognize the United States of America as a sovereign and independent nation. In 1787, it was later formalized with a treaty of Peace and Friendship, the longest standing treaty in US history.*

The cultural and historical link dates back many centuries. Our civilization was born when people first organized in cities in what is today the Arab World. These people shared similar cultures, spoke related languages, believed in similar mythologies and methods of warfare. They had many social factors in common: everything from attire to cuisine to types of dancing.

It was religion and language that shaped the Arab World. What ultimately united the land and people of what we know today by that name was the spread of Islam. It came from the Arabian Peninsula and moved across the Fertile Crescent, that territory beginning at the Mediterranean, stretching between the Tigris and Euphrates rivers, and ending at the Persian Gulf. When the Prophet Mohammad died in 632 AD, the religion could have lost its following. However, under the guidance of the first four caliphs (or successors to Mohammad), the religion spread across the entire region. Within thirty years, the Muslims had conquered Persia (Iran), Iraq, Syria, parts of North Africa, and the Byzantine (Eastern Roman) empire.

Throughout the Arab World, there are significant minorities of various faiths. For example, Lebanon is roughly 50% Christian. Morocco and Tunisia have small minorities of Jews. Members of the Coptic Christian

© 2009 Ali Farzat

Church are an important group in Egypt.

Language also served as a unifier. As the Arabs spread throughout North Africa and Southwest Asia, so did the Arabic language. Its interface with the original local languages is believed by some to have caused the evolution of dialects and regional accents.

Minority populations living in the Arab World also speak Armenian, Kurdish, Aramaic, Berber, Assyrian, Amharic and other languages. From country to country, the spoken Arabic varies quite a bit.

FYI—The Three Factor Test for determining Arab countries

*1. Cultural and historical links to each other.*

*2. One majority religion, although not the only one practiced.*

*3. One majority language, with many different dialects, although not the only one spoken.*

Arabic accents are quite diverse. A Moroccan speaking to an Omani in Arabic is similar to a Texan speaking to a Highland Scot in English. Both are speaking the same language, but because there are different word usages and pronunciation, the speakers may have a challenging time understanding one another. Speaking Modern Standard Arabic is the way around this issue.

FYI—Are there two Arabic languages?

*No. But Modern Standard Arabic (the formal version of the language that evolved from the Classical Arabic in which the Quran is written) is taught in schools, used in formal settings, in business contracts, and in most Arab Parliaments. Spoken Arabic is the less formal, colloquial version of Arabic, commonly used in everyday situations. Some would argue that it has evolved into a multitude of dialects across the Arab World.*

*Educated Arabs can understand Modern Standard Arabic, but they may have a hard time expressing themselves in it.*

While Arabic accents and dialects vary greatly from country to country, the similarities between dialects can be divided into six regional groupings.

FYI—Afghanistan

*Although Afghanistan is 99% Muslim, it is not an Arab country because Arabic is not one of its primary languages. However, many Arab and Muslim fighters who entered Afghanistan during the Soviet / Afghan war of the 1980s stayed and joined the Taliban, a group that adhered to a strict and fanatical version of Islam. The Taliban took control of Afghanistan after the Soviets pulled out and ruled it during the 1990s. Among these fighters was Osama bin Laden, a Muslim from Saudi Arabia, whose family is originally from Yemen. The bin Ladens run a multinational construction company, based in Saudi Arabia. This company has made them very wealthy. Osama bin Laden created an international terrorist network now known as Al-Qaeda. Al-Qaeda means "the base" and refers to the "database" of fighters assembled during the guerilla wars against the Soviet presence in Afghanistan. Today, a North American White Supremacist hate group is named The Base—literally, Al-Qaeda in English. Haters learn from one another.*[5]

North African Arabic, the everyday language spoken in Algeria, Morocco, and Tunisia shares many similarities, such as the inclusion of French words within it, as a result of French colonial occupation.

Egyptian Arabic has its own unique identity, but it is commonly understood by other Arabs because Cairo—Egypt's capital city—was for decades, the Hollywood of the Arab World, and the greatest producer of popular songs and singers.

East African Arabic, the language spoken in Sudan, Djibouti, the Comoros Islands, and by the minority Arabic-speaking populations of Somalia, Eritrea and Ethiopia, shares some similarities, including an intermixture of African languages.

Levantine Arabic is spoken in Jordan, Lebanon, Palestine, and Syria. While the accents vary, the vocabulary remains largely the same throughout.

In the case of Iraqi Arabic, there is a slight geographical division. The southern part of Iraq, which is close to the Arabian Peninsula, shares accents with the countries of the Gulf region, whereas the Arabic of northern and western Iraq is more closely related to Levantine Arabic.

The Arabic of the Arabian Peninsula—that is spoken in Saudi Arabia, Kuwait, Bahrain, Qatar, the United Arab Emirates, Oman, and Yemen—generally shares similarities, while retaining its own individual, at times very distinctive, accents.

Most individual cities across the Arab world have their distinct and easily recognizable accents.

Let's now apply the three criteria to some other countries in the region. Iran does share some cultural and historic similarities with the Arab World: history, attire, certain cuisine, traditions, and customs. So, Iran partially meets the cultural/historical criterion. It is also among the ten most populous Muslim countries in the world, and thus meets the religious criterion. Ethnically different from Arabs, Iranians are Aryans while Arabs are Semites. Even the root name of the country is derived from the ethnicity, Aryan = Iran. Iranians speak Farsi (known in English as Persian), not Arabic. Therefore, Iran is not an Arab country.

How about Israel? Although it shares some cultural/historical traits in terms of food, dance, and history, it does not qualify under either the majority religion criterion (which is Judaism) or the language (which is Hebrew). While there are Arabs living in Israel, it is not an Arab country. Hebrew and Arabic are both Semitic languages, you hear it in peace, "Shalom" and "Salaam", respectively, and many other words.

What about Greece? Well, it shares a lot of history and culture with the Arabs—since both peoples were ruled by the Ottoman Turks. Is it Gyro or Shawarma? Is it Baklava or Baqlawa? Is it a Kalamtianos dance or a Dabke? Eastern Orthodox Christianity is the majority religion in Greece, not Islam, and the language there is Greek. Thus, it is not an Arab country. What about Finland? Well, it doesn't meet any of the criteria, so it's immediately kicked out!

### Immigrant Arabs and Arab-Americans
As already mentioned, three to four million Arab-Americans live in the United States.

FYI—Arab-Israelis or Palestinians with Israeli Citizenship
*Roughly 20% of Israel's population is Arab and non-Jewish (typically Christian or Muslim). Some identify themselves as Palestinians with Israeli citizenship while others see themselves as Arab-Israelis. Beyond the 20%, some ethnic Arabs are Sephardi*

*or Mizrahi (Eastern) Jews. The term Sephardi originally referred to Jews of the Iberian Peninsula prior to the Spanish Reconquista. More recently, it has come to include Jews of Arab and Persian backgrounds who have no historical connection to present day Spain and Portugal. The term Mizrahi generally refers to Jewish people from the Middle East.*

About 83% of them are US citizens. While most of the Arab World is Muslim, the Arab-Americans are overwhelmingly Christian (77%). More specifically, 42% of these Christians are Catholic, 23% Eastern Orthodox (belonging to Antiochian, Greek, Russian, or Syrian Orthodox denominations), and roughly 11% are Protestant. Only 23% of Arab-Americans are Muslim. Thus, I am a double-minority as I am of Arab extraction and Muslim, while most Arab-Americans are Christian and most Muslim Americans are either African-American or South Asian. [6]

Arab-Americans live in every state in the nation and hold positions across society. They are taxi drivers and grocers, firefighters and law enforcement officers, doctors and lawyers, nurses and dentists, business executives and stockbrokers, designers and entertainers. Arab-Americans are woven into the fabric of American life and history.

**Who are Muslims and what do they believe?**
Arabs (ethnicity)—over three hundred million people located in mostly Southwest Asia and North Africa—constitute about 20% of the world's 1.8 billion Muslims (religion). Terminology note: These people are called Muslims—not Mooslims, Mohammedans, Mohamidans, Islamics, Mussulman, Musselman, and Mussulmaun. Employing the name of the Prophet to refer to Muslims (e.g. Muhammadans) is wrong and is similar to referring to Christians as Jesusites. Muslims do not worship Mohammad. Muslims are followers of Islam. Muslims believe in one God and regard their religion as a continuation of Judaism and Christianity. All three are seen as continuations of one another, or different branches on the same tree.

When I was growing up in small town West Virginia, my mother always taught me, "To be a good Muslim, you must first be a good Jew and a good Christian." That one sentence explains the heart of Islam. Islam continues the Abrahamic faiths.

FYI—The Faith of Arab-Americans

*42% Catholic*

*23% Eastern Orthodox (belonging to Greek, Russian, or Syrian Orthodox denominations)*

*11% Protestant*

*23% Muslim*

© 2009 Ali Farzat

Throughout its teachings, Islam refers to the "people of the book," meaning Muslims, Christians, and Jews, those whose monotheistic faith descends from Abraham. It does not matter whether you call the Divine Being, God, Yahweh, or Allah. It is the same Being who created the heavens and the earth, who supports good over evil, and whom believers hold as the highest power of all. I always ask if anyone knows what the term for God is in Aramaic, the original language of the Bible. Seldom do people know it is Allaha, one letter away from Arabic, because both are Semitic languages. Allah is simply the Arabic word for God. Arab Christians, say Allah, Arab agnostics, would say they are not sure if there is an Allah!

Islam originated in 610 AD when forty-year-old Mohammad, a deeply-spiritual native of Mecca, was meditating in a cave, as he often did. The Archangel Gabriel appeared before him and commanded Mohammad to recite what Muslims believe is the word of God. Over the next twenty years, Mohammad received many such revelations from Gabriel. These recitations were later compiled into the 114 chapters, or *suras*, of the *Quran*.

The *Quran* is the Muslim holy book, the same way that the New Testament is the holy book of Christianity and the *Torah* (Old Testament) the holy book of Judaism. Muslims believe the *Quran* to be the word of God. The term "Quran" is derived from the Arabic verb *iqra*, meaning to read or to recite, which is what the Archangel Gabriel commanded the illiterate Mohammad to do: to recite God's message. Muslims consider Mohammad to be the human messenger of God—and in the tradition of Biblical prophets.

*FYI—Arabs in Latin America, Arabtinos/Arabtinas?*

*Estimates vary as to the number of people of Arab descent in Latin America. Some say there are ten million; others put the figure as high as thirty million. These are the descendants of immigrants who arrived from what was then Ottoman Syria in the late nineteenth century. A friend from that background told me she and her family called themselves Arabtinos! For example, of Honduras' population of six million, roughly 200,000 are of Arab descent.[8] About 25% of the population of San Pedro Sula, Honduras' second largest city, descend from Arabs.[9] The family of Latin America's richest businessman, Carlos Slim Helú of Mexico, came originally from Lebanon. In June 2007, Senor Helú surpassed Bill Gates as the wealthiest person in the world. Two former Ecuadorian presidents, a president of Argentina, a prime minister of Belize, a minister of education of El Salvador, and a minister in Brazil were of Arab descent.[10] Latin Americans of Arab descent constitute a vital and highly-visible part of society, occupying as they do a larger proportion of the population than in the United States.*

There are the five pillars, or five required religious practices, in Islam:

1. Belief in one God, whose Messenger is Mohammad—Testament of Faith
2. Prayer five times a day (at set times)
3. Charity
4. Fasting during the holy month of Ramadan (if one is able to)
5. Pilgrimage to Mecca (if one is able to)

Moreover, there are six articles of faith:

1. Belief in God
2. Belief in the Angels
3. Belief in the Holy Books
4. Belief in the Day of Judgement and the Afterlife
5. Belief in the Prophets
6. Belief in Destiny

The best and worst thing about Islam is its fluidity and openness for interpretation. Islam does not have a formal baptismal process, you must simply believe the first pillar, the testament of faith or Shahadah and you're in, so if you read that out loud, sorry, but now you're a Muslim. Good luck checking in for your next flight! Kidding! Islam does not have any religious leader, such as the Pope, nor any ordained council. It is meant to be a religion of personal reflection and action, a direct relationship between each individual and God, unmediated by a priestly caste. Even during the time of the prophet, the message was received and interpreted in various ways.

Prayers at mosques are led by an *imam*, who, ideally, should be the congregation member who is most well-read in the community. People often turn to Islamic teachers or to imams (of their own mosque, or of larger mosques around the world) for help in interpreting the religion for themselves. Unfortunately, some of the individuals to whom they turn are ignorant of Islam. Or worse still, they might take verses of the *Quran* out of context, for political or for personal gain, thereby spreading deformed versions of this humanistic faith. Although this is a phenomenon that happens in all religions, following 9/11, the media has tended to focus on Islam alone, and on the most violent and extremist interpretations of it by these so-called religious leaders.

As with all other Scriptures, it is important not to isolate passages of the *Quran* out of context. Such passages become vague and unclear, if judged independently of other qualifying sections. The *Quran* itself addresses this very issue by saying, "Some verses are precise in meaning, they are the foundation of the Book, and others ambiguous. Those whose hearts are infected with disbelief follow the ambiguous part, so as to create dissension... No one knows its meaning except God."[13] Taking verses out of context from the *Quran* can lead to a grave misinterpretation of the religion. Extremists, who come to be considered Islamic scholars or leaders, turn people astray by doing such acts. Many non-Muslim individuals, including Western scholars and religious or political leaders, do the same thing too in order to denigrate Islam.

Here, for example, is a passage from the *Quran* often misquoted and misinterpreted to portray Islam as a violent faith: "When the sacred months are passed, slay the idolaters wherever you find them, and seize them, beleaguer them and lie in wait for them with every kind of ambush. But if they convert and observe prayer and pay the obligatory alms, then let them go their way for God is forgiving and merciful."[14] Taken out of context, it appears that God orders Muslims to act brutally. However, this verse refers to a specific historical incident, and the disavowal of a peace treaty, breached by the pagan enemies of Mohammad. In other verses of the *Quran*, God maintains, "Whoever killed a human being, except as punishment for murder or other villainy in the land, shall be deemed as though he had killed the whole of mankind."[15] Additionally, the *Quran* says, "Do not burn a plant, nor cut down a tree, nor kill an old man, nor a young child, nor a woman … nor monastery dwellers."[16] While there are sections addressing matters of violence within the *Quran*, as there certainly are in the Bible, it is important to remember that the term "Islam" is derived from the word *salaam*, which means peace. But as with every faith, individuals tend to read and interpret what they choose from its scripture.

FYI— Wahhabism

*"Wahhabism" is a term we often now hear in the media. It refers to a tiny sect of Islam, founded in the eighteenth century in what is present-day Saudi Arabia, by one Mohammad Ibn Abd al-Wahhab. His heterodox religious movement only gathered strength and influence thanks to its alliance with Mohammad Bin Saud, founder of the present ruling Saudi royal family and of the Kingdom of Saudi Arabia. The followers of al-Wahhab and those of Ibn Saud managed between them to unite the tribes of the region. Consequently, much of Wahhabi fundamentalist ideology became woven into Saudi society and culture. Al-Wahhab was the severest of fundamentalists, who believed that any evolution of Islam beyond the narrowest and most literal interpretations of Mohammad's teachings was blasphemous. Wahhab and his followers focused more on the differences between them and mainstream Muslims than on the similarities. The Wahhabis saw fit to label most other Muslims, as well as all other faiths, as lost in jahila ("ignorance"), the term Prophet Mohammad used to describe the pagan tribes of the Arabian Peninsula. Traditional Wahhabis regard themselves as the chosen ones, deeming other Muslims, as well as all Christians and Jews, as damned unbe-*

*lievers. Because of Saudi oil wealth, the Wahhabi fundamentalist message has been spread through the financing of its schools and publications, which are free. As a movement, Wahhabism is a recent and somewhat intolerant phenomenon. It runs counter to Islam's central principles of tolerance, coexistence and the pursuit of knowledge and scholarship.*[17]

Another false notion about Islam is that Muslims do not believe in Christianity and Judaism, and order the "conversion by the sword" or eradication of Christians and Jews. Muslims honor Moses and Jesus, and believe in the Immaculate Conception. In fact, the Virgin Mary is mentioned more times in the *Quran* than she is in the *Bible*—you read that right! Not that it's a competition, but if it was, we win! Kidding, it's not a competition. I made the mistake of saying that joke at a church once, and one lady was certainly not amused, fortunately, her taser missed! —thirty-four times in the *Quran* as opposed to only nineteen times in the *Bible*.[18] There is an entire chapter of the *Quran* dedicated to Mary. "Those who believe, and those who follow the Jewish scriptures, and the Christians who believe in God and the Last Day, and work righteousness, shall have their reward with their Lord; on them shall be no fear, nor shall they grieve."[19]

FYI—Sharia

*Sharia is often labeled as Islamic law, though some would argue that it is more precisely an evolving body of law inspired by the Quran and the Sunna (or the Teachings of the Prophet Mohammad). Islam can be interpreted to provide instruction for most aspects of life. Sharia is formed from two main fields: religious guidance, as well as judicial guidance on far-ranging issues that include marriage, divorce, child custody, and inheritance.*[20]

Other misguided people look for absurd examples to invoke a fear of Islam. The religious holiday of *Eid*, a term that literally means "celebration" in Arabic, has been written in reverse to spell "die." A small number of individuals actually believe that transliterating an Arabic word and rearranging the letters demonstrates how Islam is embedded with violence. Such absurdities are baseless and counterproductive to the greater good.

Point to Ponder
Key Language: "Allah" is not the Muslim God
*Allah is the Arabic word for "God." Because the Prophet Mohammad spoke in Arabic, and the Quran was sent to him in Arabic, "Allah" has become incorrectly interpreted by non-Arabic speakers as connoting the "Muslim God." However, it is important to note that all Arabic-speakers use the word to refer to God, regardless of whether they are Muslim, Christian, Jewish, atheist, or otherwise. In Aramaic, the original language of the Bible, the term for "God" is "Allaha," which is only one letter away from the Arabic "Allah."*

We are beginning to hear the newly-coined terms "*Islamists*" and "*Islamofascists*," to mean "violent extremists." These terms, while widespread, are misleading. Many people find it troublesome that a word derived from "Islam" is applied to organizations they consider radical and extreme. However, the terms "Islamist" and "Islamism" are used in publications within Muslim countries to describe domestic and transnational organizations seeking to implement Islamic law. The English website of Al Jazeera, for example, uses these terms frequently. Similarly, "*jihadi*" is a poor choice to refer to a violent extremist, because *jihad* (struggle) is justified by faith. Instead, use the term "violent extremist" when discussing such a person. By using religious sounding language, one further arms the extremists and helps justify their causes as religiously motivated and supported. In reality, they are not and can be disarmed of such influence by taking away the religious sounding terms.

## Women in Islam

Another area of Islam that is regularly misinterpreted and incorrectly practiced concerns the relationship between the sexes. Islam preaches equality between women and men. Arabic, the original language of the *Quran*, is not gender-neutral, meaning that many words have both a masculine and feminine form. As such, the *Quran* makes itself clear. For example, when discussing the believers, a verse would mention both believing men and believing women, faithful men and faithful women, pious men and pious women.

Nowhere in the *Quran* does a verse indicate that one gender is superior to the other. The *Quran* asserts, for example, that women and men were created from a single soul. "O mankind! Be careful of your duty to your Lord who created you from a single soul and from it its mate and from them both have spread abroad a multitude of men and women. Be careful of your duty toward God in whom you claim (your rights) of one another, and towards the wombs (that bore you). Lo! God has been a Watcher over you."[21] This is quite different from women being created from the rib of a man or that men were created first, both of which can imply that women are somehow inferior to men.[22]

FYI— Sunni and Shia Islam

*In recent years, the public has started to hear more about Sunni and Shia Islam. People hear buzzwords and news highlights and sometimes get confused. Put simply, Sunni and Shia are two denominations in Islam, similar to Catholic and Protestant in Christianity. There are distinctions and differences in interpretations, traditions, and beliefs, but they are still under the same umbrella of Islam.*

*All Sunnis do not hate all Shias, and all Shias do not hate all Sunnis. Similar to how all Catholics don't hate all Protestants and vice versa. Even during the conflict in Northern Ireland, the rest of the world knew better than to expand the perception of hostility to Christendom at large. The same reasoning applies with Sunni and Shia and what takes place in Iraq.*

*Simply put, the split in the faith took place after the death of the Prophet and revolved around who was best suited to succeed the Prophet and lead the people. One group that later came to be known as Sunni, wanted to nominate the leader, or Caliph— which means successor, based on who they believed to be best suited. Caliphate, literally means succession state—so the DAESH fools were literally claiming to be the rightful successors to Prophet Muhammad. Fortunately, 1.8 billion Muslims didn't buy it, but several thousand did. The percentage of those who bought in to that violent movement that claimed to be Muslim were less than half of a percent of the global Muslim populous, based on who they believed to be best suited. The other group, later known as Shia, believed it was the wish of the Prophet to continue the succession through the bloodline. Both groups have evidence to support their claims. There is no particular appearance to help settle if one is Sunni or Shia anymore than one can look at someone's appearance and determine if they are Catholic or Protestant. There was a poor and misleading Time Magazine cover in 2007 when the sectarian violence was mushrooming in Iraq where they had two men covered up in the Kufi—the traditional Arab checkered or plain scarf that has absolutely nothing to do with religion and is purely cultural—one with a red and white and one with a black one. The men's eyes are all you can see and their look is certainly ominous, they're not asking you over for some homemade falafel. "Why They Hate Each Other" states the all caps title. It's not gang colors or clothes folks! It doesn't work that way. The only physical tell is how they worship, Sunnis pray with their arms around their waste, Shias pray with their arms along their side. That's it. I've prayed in all sorts of houses of worship, including Shia mosques, and no one cared that my hand stance was that of a Sunni (I just say I'm Muslim and don't subscribe to one denomination). No one cared, no one gave me funny looks or said "Jump him… after prayer brother!"*

*Sunnis make up an estimated 90% of the Muslim population and are found all over the world. Shias make up an estimated 10% and are located heaviest in Azerbaijan, Bahrain, Iran, Iraq, Yemen, and parts of Afghanistan, Lebanon, Syria, and Turkey, but can also be found globally. Sunni is derived from the religious term sunna which speaks to the teachings of the Prophet. Shia is derived from Shiat Ali translated to mean those who are on the side of Ali. Ali was the Prophet's son-in-law. Have you heard what happens when a Sunni and a Shia get married? They end up with a Sushi kid!*

Islam advocates that men and women have exactly the same responsibilities and duties. The *Quran* teaches that men and women must be paid equally. Passages express, "Men and women have equal rights of earning"[23] and "I shall not lose sight of the labor of any of you who labors in My way, be it man or woman; each of you is equal to the other."[24] It is noteworthy that Mohammad's wife Khadija was a successful businesswoman, the primary breadwinner in the family. Islam also stresses the importance of educating both sexes. Acquiring as much knowledge as possible throughout one's lifetime is considered a virtue. According to the *Hadith*, Mohammad said that seeking knowledge is mandatory for every Muslim, man and woman. Judging Islam on the actions of the Taliban or Al-Qaeda is kin to judging Christianity on the actions of the Ku Klux Klan!

Islam does not condone or suggest the oppression of women in any way. The religion, instead, champions the independence and overall respect of women. Prior to the existence of Islam, Jewish, Christian, and pagan tribes in what is present-day Saudi Arabia captured many women as slaves and sexual objects. Islam liberated slaves of all kinds and made concerted efforts to raise women from their objectified existence. The Prophet Mohammad was anxious to emancipate women. They were among his first converts.[25] Islam gives women rights of inheritance and divorce, which women in the West did not enjoy until the nineteenth century. Islam preaches modesty of both men and women. In an effort to de-objectify themselves in the period of early Islam, converted women began wearing looser clothing and covering their hair, so as no longer to be judged by their bodies, but only their work and words.

Point to Ponder

Buzzword: Jihad

*Jihad is commonly thought of as Muslim holy war against non-Muslims. Although popularized by violent extremists and the media, this usage is incorrect. The concept of jihad does exist in Islam and means "struggle" in Arabic.*

*Within the context of Islam, there are two forms of jihad: greater jihad and lesser jihad. Greater jihad is meant to be the daily and personal struggle to be a better person, to resist temptation, to serve God, and to help one's fellow human beings. For example, when one fasts during the holy month of Ramadan, it is considered part of his struggle, his jihad.*

*Lesser, sometimes called defensive—notice the adjectives, jihad is meant to be a military stand against enemies of the religion whose goal is to attack the religion and threaten it and its followers with annihilation. A good friend of mine explains it best: If the concept of lesser or defensive jihad existed in Judaism, then Jewish uprisings against the Nazis in World War II would have been a fitting example. In my view, the most recent true example of lesser or defensive jihad occurred in the eleventh century when Salah El-Din (Saladin) fought the Crusaders. Some people have asked if defensive jihad would be justified in the Soviet/Afghan war, the genocide against the Rohingya Muslim minority in Burma or the persecution of the Uyghur Muslim minority in China.*

*Keep this in mind: When violent extremist groups like Al-Qaeda characterize their acts of violence as jihad, they are misapplying the concept and hijacking the term and the faith. Their actions are not in defense of Islam. It is in no way threatened by annihilation. Violent extremists attack innocent civilians. By initiating such action, they contradict Islam and the foundations of lesser or defensive jihad. If we use their terminology, we are empowering them and incorrectly justifying that they are indeed involved in a religious duty. (To further confuse the situation, "Jihad" is also sometimes used as a gender-neutral first name in Arabic, irrespec-*

© 2009 Ali Farzat

*tive of their faith. If you meet someone named Jihad—man or woman—it does not mean they are Muslim.)*

FYI—Hadith and Quran

*The Hadith is a collection of the teachings and sayings of the Prophet Mohammad organized and written by a specific group of his companions roughly two hundred years after his death. It is considered to compliment the Quran. The Arabic text of the Quran is believed to be the only word of God. As each text has been translated into a multitude of languages around the world, transliteration of Arabic names and some terms has proved to be challenging. "Quran," "hadith," "Mohammad" are considered now to be the standardized English spellings of each. "Quran" is pronounced core-ann. "Hadith" is pronounced ha-deeth. "Mohammad "is pronounced mo-ham-mad.*

In that early period, wearing the *hijab*, or head covering, for women became a symbol of empowerment, and it is so regarded by many women today. A recently converted woman stated that, because of wearing looser clothing and the *hijab*, "Men treat me as a person, as a professional, not as a sex object."[26] It is important to note that Islam does not require women to cover their hair outside of prayer; this is a personal choice. Women covering their hair predates Islam. Judaism encouraged the practice and even today many Orthodox Jewish women cover at least their shoulders for prayer services. In many Catholic countries today, women cover their hair when attending church.

This section explains the theoretical equality of the sexes in Islam. Unfortunately, as in other aspects of the religion, gender equality is an area in which both political and religious leaders have manipulated Islam so as to make it patriarchal and oppressive to women. In other words, they have made it conform, not to Islam, but to ancient tribal practices. Laws that hinder the independence and equality of women, such as Saudi Arabia's laws forbidding women to drive, which was finally lifted in 2018, are very much against the equality that Islam preaches. The fact that women often do not enjoy equal rights in Muslim or Arab societies has social, rather than religious, roots.

Acclaimed author, professor, and former nun Karen Armstrong adds

© 2009 Ali Farzat

some pertinent and relevant information about the position of women in religions. She states that whenever a religion was born, the position of women took a turn for the worse.[27]

Professor Armstrong states, "Most of these religions had an egalitarian ethos, but they were and have remained essentially male spiritualities. Confucius, for example, seemed entirely indifferent to women; Socrates was not a family man. In India, the Jain and Buddhist orders were irenic forms of the ancient Aryan military brotherhoods, and though nuns were permitted to join, in a second-class capacity, many felt that the presence of women was inappropriate. Even the Buddha, who did not usually succumb to this type of prejudice, declared that women would fall upon his order like mildew on a field of rice."[28]

Armstrong continues: "This chauvinism infects the spirituality of the faithful, male and female alike. Male Jews are supposed to thank God daily for not creating them women; every Christmas, Christians sing

'Lo! He abhors not the Virgin's womb,' as though Jesus's tolerance of the female body was an act of extraordinary condescension on his part."[29]

Let's look at the issue of polygamy. Polygamy has existed throughout the world for many centuries—in the Far East, in Africa, in the Arab World, and even in the United States where Mormons were polygamous up until about a century ago. (Some fundamentalist Mormons in southern Utah and northern Arizona still practice polygamy.) Polygamy became established in these societies for multiple reasons. As societies modernize, polygamy tends to disappear. In his time and place, Mohammad's restriction against a man having more than four wives was, in fact, an advance, a protection for women and their children. Moreover, in that time, women who did not have the protection of a man and his household were lost in the societies where they lived. As Muslim countries modernize, polygamy is disappearing. Very few modern Muslim men can own a house and a car, pay for their children's education, and offer equivalent accommodation to multiple wives.

Let's examine polygamy in Islam. Can a Muslim male marry up to four women? Yes, this is technically allowed. However, it is not often practiced today. Polygamy in Islam originated in the early days of the religion's existence during a time of war and ongoing battles between local and regional tribes. Because many men died in battle, the female to male ratio was much higher than usual. Consequently, the surviving men were expected to protect and care for the women. In order for the widows to live in the same household with men to whom they were not related, they had to be married. Mohammad also entered into multiple marriages to unite the tribes.

The *Quran* explains, "If you deem it best for the orphans, you may marry their mothers—you may marry two, three, or four. If you fear lest you become unfair, then you shall be content with only one, or with what you already have. Additionally, you are thus more likely to avoid financial hardship."[30] In a sense, polygamy in Islam was meant to be a form of welfare, not to provide men pleasure. *Harems*, where a ruler or a rich man has many wives, is an aberration under Islam.

Today, polygamy exists only in rare situations. When it does occur, it is usually through a selfish interpretation of the religion by men. In the Arab World, it is considered backward for a man to take multiple wives, and is very much looked down upon. Men sometimes take additional wives thinking that it legitimizes what is essentially taking a mistress.

Questions sometimes arise about the treatment of women in mosques. For instance, why do women and men sometimes enter through different doors? Why do they not pray among one another? Sometimes women are seated behind the men. Does that symbolize women as lesser than men because they are in the rear? Firstly, women are not always behind men in mosques. Depending on the design of the mosque, women are sometimes situated on the second floor, above the men, physically elevated, refuting the notion that they are subordinate. Moreover, in the mosque, a house of God, Muslims are meant to worship; nothing else. How many reading this book have been in a church or house of worship and, instead of listening to the minister or priest, were checking out someone in the congregation? Everyone who visits a mosque to worship is meant to do so without distraction.

### Global Muslim Population

Islam is the world's second most practiced religion after Christianity. The Muslim world numbers roughly 1.8 billion people, although worldwide estimates have ranged from 1.5 to 2 billion. Most Muslims live not in the Arab World, but in South Asia and the Indian subcontinent. More Muslims live in South Asia than in the entire Arab World. South Asia includes India,

Pakistan, Afghanistan, Nepal, Bhutan, Bangladesh, Sri Lanka, and Singapore. While none of these countries is Arab, each is either majority Muslim or has high numbers of Muslims within its population.

As with the "Christian World," it is difficult to describe the "Muslim World" geographically because Muslims live in every part of the world, on every continent. Islam has spread across the world. The highest concentrations of Muslims are in Africa and Asia.

FYI—Muslims in Latin America

*Islam is among the fastest growing religions in Latin America. Estimates of Muslims there reach about six million, many of them recent converts. Others are descendants of Muslims who came to the region many decades ago as slaves from Africa. While the people integrated into Latin American life, many retained their religion.*

We can confirm that none of these South Asian countries is Arab by simply applying the three factor test: (1) cultural/historical link; (2) dominant religion of Islam, although not the only one practiced; (3) dominant language is Arabic with many dialects, although not the only one spoken. Let us use Pakistan as an example. Because of

the Silk Road and the constant commerce it carried between the Arab World and South Asia, there are aspects of culture and history that overlap between it and the Arab World. However, those aspects do not constitute a strong cultural or historical link. Pakistan's dominant religion is Islam; in fact, it is one of the top ten most populous Muslim countries. Therefore, the second factor is met. Finally, the third factor, often the most determinative, is language. The Pakistani national language is English, which is used in the Constitution, corporate business dealings, and universities. The official language is Urdu, although it is only spoken by roughly 8% of the population.[31] Most Pakistanis actually speak Punjabi.[32] Pakistan hosts a number of other languages and dialects as well, as do many parts of South Asia. Arabic, however, is not spoken at all. Although many Muslims who are Pakistani may be able to read Arabic because they learned it to read the *Quran*, an ability to read Arabic does not equate with an ability to speak or fully grasp the language.

The United States is home to roughly four million Muslims, few of them Arab. The two largest groups of American-Muslims are African-Americans and South Asians. Best estimates are that 33% of mosque-attending American-Muslims are of South Asian descent and another 30% are African-American.[33] Islam continues to be one of the fastest growing religions in the world, including in the United States. That is due both to high birthrates among Muslims as well as conversion to the religion.

In short, Arabs and Muslims are two separate heterogeneous groups that overlap, but are not one and the same. Muslims are followers of the monotheistic religion of Islam that has many similarities to Judaism and Christianity. Arabs are a multiracial and diverse people who are rooted in the Arab World, which spans North Africa and Southwest Asia. Arabs practice a variety of faiths, including Islam, Christianity, and Judaism.

## Question Three

### What is the world's most populous Muslim country?

Answers to this question often reflect what Muslim countries are being discussed in the media: Iraq, Saudi Arabia, or Afghanistan. Sometimes the answer is "Africa." Africa, of course, is not a country, but a continent of fifty-three independent nations. Israel is, surprisingly, another common answer, though it is predominantly Jewish, not Muslim.

The correct answer is Indonesia, a nation of islands located in South East Asia, between Australia and Malaysia. With roughly 270 million people, Indonesia is the world's most populous Muslim country. Ninety percent of Indonesia's population is Muslim.[34] Ethnically, Indonesians are not Arabs, but overwhelmingly native people of these islands, including Javanese, Madurese, and Sundanese (not Sudanese, who are predominantly Arab).[35] Muslim merchants and traders brought Islam from the Arab World and introduced certain cultural influences to Indonesia.

The top nine most populous Muslim countries are: Indonesia, Pakistan, Bangladesh, India, Turkey, Iran, Egypt, Nigeria, and China. Of these, only Egypt is an Arab country.[36] Algeria, Morocco, and Sudan come next on this list.[37] As you can see, only four out of the top twelve most populous Muslim countries are also Arab, all on the continent of Africa.

FYI—China
*Islam in China dates to as early as 650 AD, less than twenty years after the death of the Prophet Mohammad. An envoy, sent by Uthman, the third caliph, and led by the prophet's uncle, Sa`ad ibn Abi Waqqas, was received by Yung Wei, the Tang emperor who ordered the construction of the Memorial mosque in Canton, China's first mosque. During the Tang Dynasty, China had its golden day of cosmopolitan culture. This facilitated the introduction of Islam. The first major Muslim settlements in China were composed of Arab and Persian merchants. Today, it is estimated that 1% to 2% of the population of China is Muslim.*

# Chapter Two

# What an Arab Looks Like

## Stereotypes Here and Abroad

THIS SECOND CHAPTER OF THE BOOK LOOKS briefly at both conscious and unconscious bias.

Topics to be discussed:

- Stereotypes about Arabs and Muslims.
- What does an Arab *look* like?
- Why do *they* hate *us*?
- Arab culture, advances, and inventions.

Points to Remember:

- Arabs are a very diverse people and span the spectrum in appearance.
- Arabs are responsible for a significant number of historical advances and have made serious contributions to global society.
- It is important to remember that, due to the transliteration of Arabic names, the same word in Arabic may be spelled a variety of different ways in English.
- Sikhs are neither Arab nor Muslim. Instead, they are followers of the fifth largest religion in the world, Sikhism.

As with all stereotypes, though some seeds of truth may make up a small part of the overall picture, they are generally inaccurate.

## Question Four

### What comes to mind when you hear the term Muslim or Arab?

This is my favorite question. It is so simple, yet so insightful. Take a minute and think about your answers. What is the first thing that comes to mind when you hear the term *Muslim* or *Arab*?

## What does an Arab look like?

When I ask this question in classes, often people who have no idea will start describing me. I am just under 5'8", with olive-toned skin, dark hair, and a thin beard (think Russell Crowe in the movie *Gladiator*, only shorter, darker, and not as suave). For example, people would respond, "Arabs are short." Well, no, that *I* am short does not mean that all Arabs are short. People will get uncomfortable and say things like "prominent nose", to which I snap back and clarify, "big nose!" It's ok, this is a safe space.

So what *does* an Arab look like? The typical reaction tends to be dark, brown, or olive-skinned, with dark hair, dark features, and men with thick facial hair. You say "Arab" and people have a certain image that pops into their heads. Similarly, and just as incorrect, you say "Latino" and one thinks of a certain image. In fact, I often get mistaken for Puerto Rican, not broader Latino, not Mexican, but specifically Puerto Rican. I joke in my lectures that Puerto Ricans are simply a better looking people and depending on my audience I either get the nod of approval or a lighthearted "nah, you're Bolivian, at best!" Arabs, like Latinos, cut across the racial spectrum because they are a multiracial, heterogeneous group. There are Arabs of every combination of skin tone, eye color, hair color and texture, and size and shape. While olive tones and dark hair and eyes tend to be the most common physical attributes found among Arabs, you will also find redheads, blondes, blue eyes, green eyes, white skin, black skin, and everything in between.

If a man is wearing a turban, it rarely means he is Arab. In the United States, more often, this is a sign that he is a Sikh. Sikhism (pronounced Sik-ism), the world's fifth largest religion, was founded by Guru Nanak more than five hundred years ago in the Punjab region of present-day Pakistan and northern India. Sikhism is its own separate monotheistic faith. Sikh, which means student, follow what are known as the Five K's: Kesh (uncut hair), Kangha (a wooden comb), Kara (a steel bracelet often given at entry to adulthood similar to a Bat Mitzvah or a Quinceanera), Kachera (cotton underpants), and the Kirpan (which is a ceremonial dagger, symbolizing justice.) Note, the Kirpan is not intended as a weapon anymore than a large crucifix would be a weapon. Sikhs number approximately twenty-four to thirty million people worldwide and roughly one million in North America.[38]

Unfortunately, in the post 9/11 America, Sikhs have felt a lot of the hate crimes. The Oak Creek, Wisconsin Sikh temple (known as a Gurdwara) shooting in 2012 where seven adherents were killed by a White Supremacist is but one example. Interestingly, the attacker thought he was attacking Muslims. The first hate murder after 9/11 was the execution of Balbir Singh Sodhi an American entrepreneur who was shot five times because the attacker thought he was Arab or Muslim, even if he were, it of course does not make him responsible for the 9/11 attacks on our country. Haters don't care. I often will worship at a synagogue during Islamic holidays because that's the beauty of our interfaith love. Sadly, I also often wonder if my synagogue (yes, I love saying that!) would be attacked by some hater because it's a double target Jews as well as Muslims.

I was training officers on the Northern Border a few years ago and asked for a volunteer to come up to the front of the class and drop their pants. Unfortunately for me, in those lonely snowy lands, I had three enthusiastic volunteers jump up. My exercise had backfired, but generally, people in our society do not feel comfortable dropping their pants in public. It's shameful. It's private. On a related note, for a Sikh male covering their hair or a Muslim woman doing the same feel that same immodesty and shame if their hair is exposed.

On a lighter note, similar to how so many people know the Islamic greeting of peace "Asalamo Alaikoum"—which can be said to any Muslim or since the language is Arabic can be said to any Arab speaker, irrespective of their faith. In Sikhism, the greeting phrase is Punjabi for "God is true and timeless" or Sat-Sri-Akal. If you say such phrases to the respective community members you will not only break the ice, you'll melt the glacier. I practice what I preach and one day, I decided to offer that Sikh greeting to a local cashier at a local business that I knew from his beard and turban style was Sikh. I was poised and excited and as my turn came up to checkout, I said it. "Sat-Sri-Akal"… now, he was probably thinking, why is this Puerto Rican speaking Punjabi to me, but the deed was done. He smiled, asked if I was Sikh and we had an instant bond. Communication + Understanding = Trust.

This reminds me of a good story about stereotypes. I once had a police officer genuinely and in all seriousness ask me, "Where's your turban?" I paused, looked at her with a big smile, and asked her back, "Where's your cowboy hat?" Immediately, she started laughing and the absurdity of her question was suddenly clear to her. It is worth noting that Arab turbans are purely cultural, whereas Sikh turbans are a religious article and eventually, one learns to identify the difference in appearance.

### Nicknames and Transliteration of Names

My name, Nawar, is spelled only one way in Arabic. My name transliterated into English can be spelled in a range of ways, Nawar, Nowar, Noar, Nawer, Nawor, Noir (people ask if my name means "black" in French, I clarify that it actually means "bright" in Arabic). I tell Starbucks baristas No-R, because it's just easier, can you blame me?

Nicknames for Arabs are an interesting area of the culture. Here in the United States we shorten names (for example, Mike as short for Michael or Jen as short for Jennifer). Arabs will often be nicknamed "father of…" (*Abu*) or "mother of…" (*Imm* or *Um*). This nickname is given once a person has his or her first child. In my family, you might call my father *Abu Kareem*, as my older brother was the firstborn in our family. If a person does not have children, he or she may still have a similar, friendly nickname. For example, my nickname growing up was *Abu Nour*, meaning "Father of Light." This was because my name, Nawar, which means "bright one," is derived from *Nour*, the Arabic word for light. Arab names also use *"ibn," "bin,"* and *"bint,"* meaning "son of" and "daughter of," respectively. In Dutch, "Van" plays a parallel purpose. This is similar to many English surnames: Richardson is derived from Son of Richard. In Arabic, it would be *Bin* Richard. Thus, I will respond to several monikers, Nawar, Abu Nour, Abu Jawad (my son's name), and every so often… Batman.

Mohammad is the most popular name in the world. As a sign of respect to the Prophet, as well as a blessing for that child, many Muslims give their son the first or middle name of Mohammad. It is not uncommon for parents to name one son (or even each of their sons) Mohammad. However, none of the sons would actually go by that name but rather by the second name. As with most Arabic names, Mohammad can be spelled a variety of ways in English, Mohammed, Mohamed, Muhamed, Mahamed. Variations of Mohammad are also extremely popular; these include Ahmed, Mahmoud, Mehmet (often a tell, that the person is of Turkish extraction), and Hamid. Similarly, many women in the Western world have the names Mary or Maria, and variations include Mary Pat, Mary Jane, Marybeth, Maria Martha, Rosa Maria, and so forth.

Muslim names often refer to "worshiper" as in "Worshiper of God"— Abed Allah. Since there are ninety-nine callings of God in Islam, any one can be part of a name. For example, Abed Al-Latif means "Worshiper of The Pleasant One"; Abed Al-Azziz means "Worshiper of The Mighty One." Frequently, these extravagant names are shortened to simply Abed (worshiper) or a combination of the names such as Abed Allah (worshiper of God) becoming Abdallah.

Many Arab last names start with *Al* or *El*, meaning "the." This can be rendered several ways in English. Members of the El Rifaey family, for instance, might use Elrifaey, El'Rifaey, El-Rifaey, or even simply Rifaey. For the sake of simplicity, Arabs frequently drop the *Al* or *El* when immigrating to the United States. However, when they say their names aloud, the *Al* or *El* is still present. Arabic names often have meaning. The same way Native American names have distinct meaning, so do Arabic names. It is vital to note that the meanings are not necessarily descriptive. For example, "Fadi Al Tayeb" means "The saviour and good one."

In regard to question four (What is the first thing that comes to mind when you hear the term "Muslim" or "Arab"?), people answer in three distinct ways: extreme negatives, broad neutrals, and extreme positives. In the following section, I will elaborate on each of these categories. As the overwhelming majority of answers I receive are broad neutrals, let's begin here.

### *Muslims & Arabs:* **Broad Neutral Answers**

Often these neutral answers are clearly derived from varied media portrayals. For example: "sand," "rich," "turban," "Bedouin," "oil," "sheik," "harem," "taxi driver," "7-Eleven," "Slurpee," (Yes, I had a police officer actually say, "slurpee"!) "Middle East," "fez," "gas station attendant," "Islam," "Saudi Arabia," "camels," (It's funny, I often get "camels", but seldom hear any mention of "Arabian horses") and "Aladdin."

"Sand," "rich," "oil," and "Bedouin" are all stereotypes about Muslims and Arabs. Some people imagine the Muslim and Arab Worlds as a giant desert, with cities and villages scattered randomly throughout. Though a conventional image of many people, this is, of course, a very incomplete picture of the regions. There are vast deserts in the Arab World (and some pretty amazing desserts, but I digress), and in parts of those deserts

Bedouins and nomads live. However, supposing that this predominates would be like saying that the United States is made up of country towns run by cowboys.

The topography and climate of both the Muslim and Arab Worlds are as diverse as the people. There are beaches, dense forests, mountains that are snowcapped year-round, large metropolises, and every imaginable climate. Moreover, not every Arab country possesses oil. There are potentially more oil reserves in Alaska than in Saudi Arabia. The stereotype of the oil-rich Arab leads to assumptions of the financially rich Arab. There are rich Arabs just as there are rich Americans and other rich people all over the world. The notion that all Arabs are rich is no more accurate than supposing that all African-Americans are athletic, that all Asians are smart, and that all Caucasians are successful. These positive stereotypes may contain a kernel of truth but are untrue when applied without distinction to the entire group.

FYI—Bedouins

*The word "Bedouin" is derived from the Arabic word badawi, a generic name for a desert dweller. "Bedouin" is a term generally applied to Arab nomadic groups, who are found throughout most of the desert belt extending from the Atlantic coast of the Sahara via the Western Desert, Sinai, and Negev to the eastern coast of the Arabian desert. The term is occasionally used to refer to non-Arab groups as well, notably the Beja of the African coast of the Red Sea.*

*Bedouins were traditionally divided into related tribes, each led by a sheikh. Traditionally, they herded camels, sheep, and goats while riding on highly prized horses, moving according to the seasons for grazing lands. For centuries up to the early twentieth century, Bedouins were known for their fierce resistance to outside government and influence. Some notable Bedouin groups in Africa include the Baggara of Sudan and Chad, the Chaamba of Algeria, and the Beni Hassan of Mauritania.*[39]

As for the first thing that comes to mind being Islam, remember that people often confuse Muslims and Arabs and make the mistake of equating the two. While there is overlap between Muslims and Arabs, they are nonetheless distinct. Furthermore, while most Arabs are Muslim, only about 20% of Muslims are Arab.

"Sheik" and "harem," other responses, are aspects of the seductive allure of Muslim or Arab culture. They come out of popular stories such as *1001 Arabian Nights, Aladdin and the Magic Lamp*, flying carpets, and the legend of *Scheherazade*. Moreover, there is the image of the dominant patriarchal figure with a harem of willing, scantly clad (yet veiled) women at his beck and call. Such sheiks and harems do not actually exist anymore.

"Taxi driver," "gas station attendant," the convenience store 7-Eleven and its popular Slurpee beverage are other neutral responses based on respondents' personal experiences, or from pop culture depictions of Muslims or Arabs in the United States. Are there Muslim or Arab taxi drivers, gas station attendants, and 7-Eleven employees? Absolutely! Do most Arabs living in the United States fit into one of those three categories? Absolutely not! Muslims and Arab-Americans tend to be a highly educated group contributing to a very diverse workforce. Of Arab-Americans, 84% have achieved at least a high school diploma, more than 40% have a bachelor's degree or higher (compared to only 24% of the general public), and 15% have a post-graduate degree, nearly twice the national average of 9%. Of the school-age population, 13% are in pre-school, 58% in kindergarten through twelfth grade, 22% in college, and 7% pursuing graduate studies.[40]

As for Muslims Americans, per the Pew Research Center, about 31% have college degrees and 11% hold postgraduate degrees. On average, Muslims immigrants are more highly educated than US-born Muslims.[41]

Muslims and Arab-Americans work as taxi drivers, grocers, doctors, lawyers, comedians, actors, firefighters, police officers, FBI agents, soldiers, chefs, bus drivers, researchers, business people, teachers, engineers, and as many other professionals representing every walk of life in American society. While 5% of Arab-American adults are unemployed, about 73% of them are in the labor force, about three quarters employed in managerial, professional, technical, sales, or administrative fields. Nearly half as many work in service jobs (12%) compared to Americans overall (27%). Most Arab-Americans work in the private sector (88%); 12% are government employees.[42]

"Saudi Arabia" and "Middle East" are common responses because some people assume that Saudi Arabia represents the whole of the Arab World. But Saudi Arabia is merely one of its twenty-two diverse Arab countries. Each country is different. Few Arabs in the region share similarities to those living specifically in Saudi Arabia. While "Middle East" is a common response, that colonial term, used regularly but incorrectly as synonymous to the Arab World, represents the nations in Southwest Asia, many of them Arab. However, the Arab World stretches across North Africa.

"Camels" is another common response. Horses are rarely mentioned, although Arabian horses are known to be some of the purest and fastest in the world. Famous for needing little water and thus well-adapted to desert regions, camels do exist in the Arab World. They have played a vital role in the history and the shaping of the region. But so have horses.

Some respondents mention the fez, a headdress, usually red in color, that actually comes from ancient Turkey. It was popularized in parts of the Arab World in the nineteenth century as a status symbol of gentlemen of the Ottoman Empire. Today, one might see an older man wearing a fez, but it is a rarity outside of the tourist industry, where bellhops and porters wear traditional clothing for show.

### *Muslims & Arabs:* **Extreme Negative Answers**

The second most common category of answers are the extreme negative ones. Sometimes experience serves as a basis for judgment. Other times, unfortunately, these negatives are simply hateful epithets used to hurt or attack one's background. Examples of the extreme negatives include: "terrorist," "sand nigger," "sand monkey", "dune coon", "camel jockey," "rag head," "diaper head," "suicide bomber," and "America-hater." I have, literally, been called all of these terms. It's worth noting, that hate and bigotry aren't always so overt. I've also been denied an RV rental and felt the need to justify that I would not do any harm to it or with it. Even though the rental was available, the owner said it needed maintenance, I assured him I was worthy and just taking my child on a vacation during Covid. A week later, he reached back out asking if I still wanted the rental (What happened to the maintenance?!) and I kindly declined. I've had job offers "tabled" at a large unnamed consulting firm—in fact, I think it's still tabled from 2013—when the powerbroker saw my name and only my name. I had a nosy neighbor friend me on social media and show up to vet me when I first moved into my neighborhood. It happened to be Ramadan and he clearly wanted to see if I was fasting. My diplomacy gave in and I was respectful and answered all his intrusive questions. Another time, I was in a high-level briefing with leadership and a person's name came up on screen: Jafaar. The second most senior person in the room's natural reaction was to sing the line from Aladdin, "Jafaar, Jafaar he's our man, if he can't do it...great." I sat in silence. Others later approached, expressing their disapproval, and urging me to file a claim. I complained, but nothing came of it. No apology, no acknowledgement. Nothing. As with so many people of color or religious minorities do, I have stories.

## Epithets

"Sand nigger," "sand monkey", "dune coon", "camel jockey," "rag head," and "diaper head" are all commonly heard, hateful racial epithets directed at Arabs or those perceived to be Arab. These degrading terms are based on ignorance and hatred. "Sand nigger" and "dune coon" are an extension of the racial epithets often given to African-Americans.

"Camel jockey" goes back to the false belief that camels populate the Muslim or Arab worlds to the extent that each person owns his or her own camel. While the term does not sound derogatory, it is used in a fashion to humiliate and degrade. Similarly, mispronouncing Arab as "Ay-rab" or Muslim as "Muzie" is considered very offensive. Like the derogatory label "whitey," a variant of "white," "Ay-rab" and "Muzie" have been used in an insulting manner and have become racially and religiously charged insults.

"Rag head" and "diaper head" refer to the stereotypical image of Muslims or Arabs wearing turbans. Some Muslims and Arabs do wear various kinds of turbans. However, believing that all Muslims or Arabs wear turbans is as untrue as the stereotype that all Americans wear baseball caps or cowboy hats. These two unfortunate epithets are also used by some to refer to individuals from Southeast Asia.

Next, let's explore the stereotype that all Muslim or Arabs hate America. As an Arab-American, Muslims, and a patriot, I find this stereotype particularly disheartening and discouraging. Remember, most Americans are not "purely" American. The term Arab helps define what kind of American I am. We have Anglo-Americans, African-Americans, Asian-Americans, Latino-Americans, and so forth. America is a nation of immigrants. Except for Native Americans, we—or our ancestors—all came from somewhere else.

Do some Muslims or Arabs hate the United States? Yes, absolutely. Do most or even a large percentage of them hate us? Absolutely not. They may resent our foreign policy, but not our country. In fact, they idealize us. US culture dominates global culture today, even in the Muslim and Arab Worlds. Generally speaking, Muslims or Arabs love all things American. They want to wear our clothes, drink our soft drinks, eat our food (including fast food), drive our cars, listen to our music, watch our movies, and learn English, which has become the international language. However, a small percentage of highly conservative, traditional, perhaps puritan, Muslims regard US pop culture as sharing similarities to pagan cults of the past that worshiped money and sex.[43] This is not unlike some of the growing puritan movements within Western culture.

A survey conducted by the Pew Forum on Religious and Public Life showed that most Muslims in America were happy and fit, dare I say, normally within our society.[42] Apart from that, do many Arabs and Muslims resent the US government specifically for its foreign policy? Of course. They resent the war in Iraq. They resent the perception that, in the Arab-Israeli conflict, the United States portrays itself as both an honest broker of peace and a "special friend" to Israel. They resent the perception—whether true or not—that we are global bullies. Generally, Muslims and Arabs make a clear distinction between the American people and the nation, on one hand, and the US government and foreign policy on the other. Despite the fact that we the people elect the government, Arabs distinguish between the policies with which they disagree and Americans as individuals, because for so many of them, they do not live in democracies and see a clear distinction between the people and the politics.

Ask any US citizen who has traveled to the Muslim or Arab Worlds as a civilian how they were treated and whether they felt any overt hatred. I'll bet their experience was positive, non-confrontational, and, in fact, friendly and hospitable. Generally, Muslim and Arab cultures tend to be heavily based on generosity, hospitality, and respect.

## Terrorism

"Terrorist" is the most common extreme negative answer. It is also the most challenging to address because peoples' emotions are linked to the word. "Terrorist," one who terrorizes, bombs innocent people, and kills women and children, is a scary word, used so much that we have become desensitized to its meaning. This term is clearly associated with horrible acts in recent history: countless attacks by DAESH/ISIS against France, the United Kingdom and other US allies; the attacks on the World Trade Center and the Pentagon on September 11, 2001; the 1993 World Trade Center bombing; the USS Cole Bombing; and the attacks on US embassies in Kenya and Tanzania in 1998. All were terrible acts carried out by Arabs who proclaimed themselves Muslims.

The fact that individual Muslims or Arabs were responsible for these acts of terrorism does not mean that all Muslims or Arabs are responsible for them, nor that all Muslims or Arabs condone them. Terrorists are not only Arab or Muslims; they come in every imaginable shape and creed: pure-bred American ultra-conservatives who perpetrated the 1995 Oklahoma City bombing; Catholics of the Irish Republican Army; white supremacists who lynched blacks in the American South; African guerrillas combating apartheid in South Africa and White Afrikaner Dutch Reformed extremists trying to maintain it; the Janjaweed in Darfur. The acts of a few individuals of any group do not represent the group as a whole. There are bad Muslims and Arabs, just as there are bad individuals in every ethnic or religious group. It is not only unfair to stigmatize all Arabs and Muslims. More importantly it is also an inefficient and unproductive form of law enforcement. Terrorism is not and has never been exclusive to Arabs and Muslims.

In the past two decades, with all the terrorism that has taken place, the one largest group of victims of terror has been Muslims. When a bombing takes place in Pakistan, our media will often mention the innocent Westerners killed and forget about the local population. They are innocent victims too. Terrorism is a global dilemma that supersedes any one group, any one religion, any one people. DAESH (ie, ISIS/ISIL) slaughtered and beheaded many innocent Syrians and Muslims before the James Foley murder brought attention to the atrocities. DAESH, which is the acronym for the group in Arabic came on the international scene in 2014. We discuss them in detail in my seminars, compare and contrast them to Al-Qaeda and learn how they truly have nothing to do with Islam as they continue to try to hijack the faith.

Moreover, per the Department of Homeland Security and the FBI, the greatest threat to our homeland today stems from domestic terrorist and Homegrown Violent Extremists (HVEs)—these can include lone actors that sympathize with DAESH or AQ, but many are racially or ethnically motivated violent extremists (RMVEs) with racial, ideological, or anti-government stances.[45]

## A Bit of History

Traditional terrorism is associated with nineteenth-century, bomb-throwing revolutionaries and ethno-nationalists operating within the declining Russian, Ottoman, and Hapsburg empires. Prior to these came a series of historical acts that, in today's standard, would qualify as terrorism, ranging from Guy Fawkes, who failed in his attempt to kill King James I of England in 1605 and instate a Catholic monarch, to *La Terreur* in 1794, where radicalized rival factions during the French Revolution took out their rage on monarchs, clergy, and the public.

Terrorism intensified and became a global phenomenon, however, in the years following 1945. The Jewish Irgun in Palestine, the EOKA movement in Cyprus, and the FLN in Algeria can all be classified as the first wave of post-war, anti-colonial terrorism. Because these organizations were understood as having led to the foundation of new states by the 1960s, terrorism was seen as an effective instrument to be used by other aggrieved individuals. As many analysts have observed, terrorists use instruments of violence out of weakness. They lack the power to effect change. Some strategists have called this "displacement." That is, states and state-supported NGOs, such as Al-Qaeda, realize that they are incapable of winning or even waging a "regular" or a "conventional" war.[46]

Terrible undertakings are constantly acted out in the name of religion—and not only by Muslims in the name of Islam. In the past few years, a number of horrible attacks took place in the false name of religion. In 2001, the FBI arrested two high-ranking members of the Jewish Defense League for plotting to blow up the largest mosque in Los Angeles, California, the offices of the Muslim Public Affairs Council, and the office of Congressman Darrel Issa, who is of Christian Lebanese descent.[47] In 2002, twenty thousand Hindus attacked and killed some six hundred Muslims in the Gujarat region in India.[48] In 2004, a mob of Buddhists attacked and vandalized six Christian churches in Sri Lanka.[49]

There are so-called "bad apples" in every religion or faith, and from every background or ethnicity. It is up to the rest of us to right their wrongs, to educate and reach out to each other.

The other primary extreme negative response is "suicide bomber." Like "terrorist," this term is charged by real-life circumstances. The 9/11 hijackers were suicide bombers, and we are, unfortunately, hearing regular news accounts of suicide bombings in Israel, Palestine, Afghanistan, Pakistan, and Iraq. Violent extremist suicide bombers, whether they are Arab or not, have reinterpreted aspects of Islam to legitimize and even prize such actions. However, suicide is a major taboo in Islam. Karen Armstrong, a theologian and expert on Islam, summed it up best in an interview with *Newsweek* magazine after 9/11:

*Newsweek*: "We have all heard that suicide bombers believe they will go straight to heaven and enjoy a paradise of milk and honey, with seventy-two beautiful virgins for every martyr. Is there any religious basis for this?"

*Armstrong*: "It is completely illegitimate. The *Quran* and Islamic law forbid suicide in the strongest terms. You may not wage a war against a country where Muslims are allowed to practice their religion freely. You may not kill children or women in any war. It's a cheapened version of it to imagine these martyrs as thinking that they're buying a first-class ticket to heaven where they'll enjoy all of these virgins. Martyrdom is something done to you and you must never take anyone else with you. But what annoys me somewhat [is that] none of these questions were asked in 1995 after eight thousand Muslims were killed by Christian Serbs. We knew enough about Christianity that to say Christianity condoned the massacre, was illegitimate. The trouble is that most Western people just don't know enough about Islam to make that correct judgment."[50]

The idea of martyrdom in Islam is the same as in other religions: dying at the hand of enemies for the adherence of your faith. Martyrdom does not include ramming a plane into a building and killing oneself and thousands of others. Moreover, the whole idea of acquiring seventy-two virgins is either completely negated or explained in an equivocal context. The following excerpt explains in detail:

"Another point of contention for many Christian leaders," writes Karen Armstrong, "is Islam's presentation of Heaven as a seductive, sensuous garden of delights, where believers are promised seventy or seventy-two virgins, also called *houris,* and one can drink from rivers of wine. The fact of the matter is that the idea of heaven in the Islamic tradition is still a contentious point that has been debated for hundreds of years. Syro-Aramaic scholars, who are some of the most respected scholars of Islam, approach this issue from a linguistic perspective. Many Aramaic scholars maintain that the word *houri* is derived from the word *hur,* which means clear or pure [or free]. The three or four verses of the *Quran* that detail the idea of houris as fair maidens fail to conform to the passages before and after them, in that these passages describe fruits and beauty and other aesthetic wonders. Linguistic experts, Muslim as well as non-Muslim, believe that these verses are about fruit or intellectual purity.

"Other scholars believe that 'houri' may indeed be translated correctly as 'fair maiden,' but that this representation is allegorical [or figurative], as is every other description of Heaven in the *Quran.* After all, what use would anyone have for low-hanging fruit, palaces, and rivers of wine? And how would it be possible to describe the flavor of chocolate to one who has never tasted it? Heaven, these scholars maintain, is a place where needs are fulfilled and sorrow is no more. The allegories of the houri, the fruit, and opulence are symbolic representations of a world where physical and spiritual needs are finally fulfilled, as opposed to the world in which we live right now."[51]

I hope this helps shed some light about any confusion regarding suicide bombings as well as the constant intrigue over the supposed Islamic promise of seventy-two virgins. I'll spare you the joke about the seventy-two Virginians!

© 2009 Ali Farzat

FYI—Arab Christians and Jews

*Historically, many Jews and Christians were ethnically Arab. They worked together with Arab Muslims and coexisted in the Islamic empire—the equivalent of a global superpower. This is still true today with ethnically Arab Jews and Christians living all over the world. While there are occasional tensions and negative examples, it is still possible to walk down a street in Damascus and find mosques, churches, and synagogues. In a number of historical examples, it is worth noting Jews preferred to live in Muslim societies rather than Christian ones because they were better treated.*

## *Muslims & Arabs*: **Extreme Positive Answers**

Now let us switch to the most infrequent group of answers, the extreme positives. These responses put a smile on my face because often the rest of the class is completely unaware of them. Examples of these include: "zero," "algebra," (which I often say belongs in the negatives, right below terrorism!), "first alphabet," "the code of law," "numerals," "astronomy," and "civilization."

Let us start with the advances in mathematics. The term "algebra" is derived from the Arabic term *al-jabr*, which means "the reunion of broken parts." It uses variables and is defined as: "a mathematical system using symbols, esp. letters, to generalize certain arithmetical operations and relationships. (Ex.: $x + y = z$.)" Muslims and Arabs also made advances in trigonometry, fractions, and geometry.

Another great historical achievement is the zero. As defined by the *Merriam-Webster Dictionary*, zero is, "The arithmetical symbol 0 or null denoting the absence of all magnitude or quantity."[52] Without the concept of zero many calculations would be impossible to make. The term zero is derived from the Arabic word *sifr*, from *zefira*, and was carried over from India to the West by the Arabs. As successful merchants, Arabs traveled across the known world, spreading ideas and possessions, and bringing other such effects back with them.

Point to Ponder
Nothingness
*By around 300 BC, the Babylonians had started to use a basic numeral system and utilized two slanted wedges to mark an*

*empty space. However, this symbol did not have any true function other than as a placeholder. The use of zero as a number was a relatively late addition to mathematics. It is alleged that Indian mathematicians introduced it as early as 628 AD, after which it made its way westward. Then under the Arab Muslim beacon, Andalusia, the zero was introduced to Europe. It is speculated that the origin of a base-10 positional number system used in India is traced to China. Because the Chinese Hua Ma system is also a positional base-10 system, Hua Ma numerals—or numeral system similar to it—may have been the inspiration for the base-10 positional numeral system that evolved in India.*

*This numeral system had reached the Middle East by 670 AD. Muslim mathematicians working in what is now Iraq were already familiar with the Babylonian numeral system, which used the zero digit between nonzero digits, so the more general system would not have been a difficult step. In the tenth century AD, Arab mathematicians extended the decimal numeral system to include fractions, as recorded in a treatise by Abu'l-Hasan Al-Uqlidisi in 952-953.*

It is unclear exactly what role Arabs played in developing the numeric system. However, today Arabic numerals are the most widely used system in the world. These were probably developed in the Indian subcontinent. However, it was the Arabs who spread this system through their mercantile trade. As a result, these numerals have come to be known as Arabic numerals. This system is used everywhere in the world. We were embarrassed globally in 2019 when a survey was conducted by an American market research company, Civic Science, and then publicized by several news outlets, here and abroad, where 56% of respondents were against "teaching Arabic numerals in US schools." Oops! Too late. Let's go back to Roman numerals, wait, and then let's use those numerals in Algebra. XVIII x Y = XC?

Sometime near 670 AD in Baghdad, (which was a cultural and intellectual hub, where Arab, Greek, Persian, and Indian scholars coordinated their academic efforts), an Indian scholar introduced a predecessor of the current numbering system, the concept of one symbol representing one number, to which the Arab scholars later assigned their own numbers.[53]

*© 2009 Ali Farzat*

Some theorists believe the Arabic numerals were based on trigonometry and angles, with each numeral representing each number, based on how many angles exist in each symbol. For example, number two would have two angles, number seven would have seven angles, and so forth.[54] This concept makes logical sense because, for centuries, the Arab World excelled in discovering and broadening new ideas in mathematics.[55]

Point to Ponder
Mathematical Advances
*Abu Abdullah Mohammad Ibn Musa al-Khwarizmi (780 – 845 AD) was a mathematical pioneer and author whose work was essential to the development and advancement of mathematics.*

*He was born in the town of Khwarizm in what is now Uzbekistan. His family moved soon afterward to an area near Baghdad where he accomplished most of his work in the period between 813 and 833. Though his native language was Farsi, al-Khwarizmi published most of his scientific works in Arabic, the scientific language of his time and place. He developed the concept of the algorithm in mathematics, and the word "algorithm" itself comes from an English corruption of his last name. Al-Khwarizmi also made major contributions to the fields of algebra, trigonometry, astronomy, geography, and cartography.*

*Al-Khwarizmi's systematic and logical approach to solving linear and quadratic equations gave shape to the discipline of algebra, a word that is derived from the name of his 830 book on the subject, Hisab Al-Jabr Wal-Muqabala. While his major contributions were the result of original research, he also did much to synthesize the existing knowledge in these fields from Greek, Indian, and other sources, stamping them with his unique mark of logic and rigor. He appropriated the place-marker symbol of zero. He is also responsible for the use of Arabic numerals in mathematics that forever changed the way the world thinks about numbers.*

Now that we have learned to blame Arabs for not only algebra, but also fractions, it's time to move on to a safer subject: the first alphabet. Although ideas were put on clay tablets for thousands of years in the form of pictographs and cuneiform writings, the first actual alphabet is widely believed to have come from a city-state in present-day Syria called Ugarit. This took place at approximately 1400 BC. An original piece of the clay tablet lies in the National Museum of Damascus, in Syria.

The code of law is another very important accomplishment. We often think correctly of the Roman Emperor Justinian as the father of the civil code, circa 529 AD. However, the father of the codification of law, the basis for written, organized laws of justice in society was the Babylonian King Hammurabi (who ruled an area that comprises present-day Iraq) in roughly 1700 BC. Moreover, the very first written law is attributed to the Mesopotamian king, Urukagina, in the twenty-fourth century BC.

Point to Ponder
Old Arabs?
*It is very important to note that the people of many of these ancient cultures, such as Mesopotamia, did not necessarily speak Arabic. However, they were the historic ancestors of today's Arabs. They were all people of the land.*

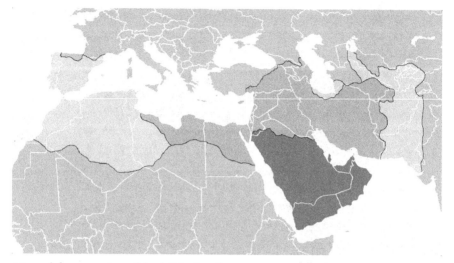

*Map of the expansion of Arab/Muslim Empires*

One of the positive results of Arab advances in science is astronomy. During the peak of the Muslim Arab empire from the eighth through the thirteenth centuries, great advances were made in astronomy. Knowledge of the stars was important to these Muslim Arabs to help them track time in order to identify hours for prayer. Additionally, they needed proper navigation skills in order to direct their prayer toward Mecca. This was one of the driving forces behind a number of broad advances within astronomy, including the compass, the astrolabe, nautical maps, and seaworthy lanterns. The Arab influence on astronomy is evident when looking up at the stars. What are Rigel and Betelgeuse in the constellation of Orion? They are transliterations from the Arabic of *rijl* (foot, as it is literally the foot of the giant Orion) and *bat el jouza* (shoulder of the giant). How about Saiph? It means *sword* in Arabic. Every star in Cygnus has an Arabic root. Many more names derived from Arabic exist in astronomy.

FYI—Where is Mesopotamia?
*Ancient Mesopotamia rests in present-day Iraq and Syria. It was one of many great empires that have controlled this part of the world over the past six thousand years.*

Finally, there is the achievement of the broader concept of civilization—specifically, the Islamic civilization that contributed so much to the world and ushered in the Renaissance. While Europe was experiencing its Dark Ages, the Arab and Muslim Worlds were at the peak of their golden age, which lasted from approximately the seventh century until the fifteenth century. The reach of this golden age spanned from present-day Spain and Portugal all the way to Central Asia. During this period, Arabs translated previously lost Greek and Roman works of science and literature, and expanded their findings. They made a range of advances in global society that helped plant the seeds of the eventual Renaissance and still make an impact today. Ok, so here's my movie idea, imagine a graphic novel style storyline like the film *300*. In 711 (No, that's not why the stores are called that!), a Christian chief from Toledo, Spain, not Ohio, sent an emissary to Damascus—the capital of the Umayyad Empire - to ask for help and protection from the northern European Visigoths who were oppressing them. The Umayyad's agreed and sent a one-eyed Berber general named Tarek Bin Zyad to save them. He crossed Gibraltar (a poor transliteration of his name meaning "Mount Tarek") and in a crazy, yet badass move, torched the ships on the beach and proclaimed, "The sea is behind us, and the enemy is in front of us, and there is only one way out." They attacked the Visigoths and killed King Roderick in battle and that was the birth of Andalusia, where for eight centuries people flocked to study and learn and exchange ideas...in Arabic. On January 2, 1492 (more than one thing happened that year), King Ferdinand and Queen Isabella kicked out the remaining Jews and Muslims, but a lot of the Arabic language stayed behind. So today, we have about 4000 words in Spanish, 1000 in English, and 900 in French derived from Arabic. Know someone named Alvarez? Pretty common name, it's a descripto, litterally "The Knight" Al-Faris! So cool! If anyone asks you if you speak Arabic, say yes, and respond back with any one of the variety of words. Admiral is the commander of the sea, correct? That's literally what it means "Amir el Bahr". So many examples, you can see why this topic is so exciting for me. Some additional advances and contributions from the Arab Muslims include:

- Alcohol (derived from Arabic *al kuhoul*)[56]
- Algorithms[57]
- Backgammon[58]
- Crystallized sugar[59]

- Compass[60]
- Coffee[61]
- Cotton[62]
- *El Taleb*, which means "the yearning one" or "the student." It is the Arab equivalent to *The Kama Sutra*. The Arabs had a hedonistic view of sex, viewing it as for pleasure as well as procreation.[63]
- Hookah[64], also known as Hubbly-Bubbly, Argilla, Nargilla, or Chi Cha
- Hydrolics[65]
- Introduction of varied fruits and cultivation to Europe[66]
- Lute (the predecessor of the guitar)[67]
- Medical advances, including eye surgery and anesthesia[68]
- Navigation Maps[69]
- Pendulum[70]
- Syrup[71]
- Universities[72]
- Translation and preservation of Greek and Roman literature[73]

FYI—The Umayyad Empire and the Umayyad Mosque
*The Umayyads (also known as Umawiy depending on the transliteration of the term from Arabic into English) were an Arab Muslim dynasty responsible for one of the greatest and largest empires in history. At its peak, the empire stretched from the borders of China, throughout North Africa, and into Southern Europe. Their rule was based in Damascus where they built the great Umayyad Mosque, which was replicated throughout their empire. Interestingly, the mosque is situated on land that has always been sacred. Initially built as a pagan temple, it was later dedicated as a Roman temple to the sun god and still later expanded as a church. With the rise of Islam, Muslims worshiped next to their Christian brethren at this church. Once the numbers grew so much, the Caliph asked permission from the Christian community to purchase the land and expand it into a great mosque. In return for the right to purchase, he also built a new church in Damascus.*

Of course, this is only a summary of some of the advances and inventions that led to a thriving civilization within the Arab and Muslim world. The Arabs also learned and spread advances from other civilizations. They successfully absorbed and honed talent from all over the known world. Arabs took paper from the Chinese and, while learning from the Chinese, seem to have been the first to use gunpowder for propulsion in battle. Similar to the United States' present global dominance, the Arab Muslim world was the dominant global power for roughly eight hundred years. The world spoke Arabic and people came from all over to learn, research, and absorb knowledge in the Arab World. In the way that our modern-day university system hosts students from all over the world, so did universities in Cordoba, Cairo, Damascus, and Baghdad. In numerous cases, non-Arabs or non-Muslims made advances in the intellectual haven of the Arab/Muslim golden age. Jews, Hindus, and Christians lived and studied in peace with their Muslim hosts. Furthermore, Indians, Persians, and Italians lived and studied with their Arab colleagues.

© *2009 Ali Farzat*

# Chapter Three

# Racial Profiling

## Morality vs Effectiveness

THIS THIRD CHAPTER OF THE BOOK EXPLORES the problems that arise when racial profiling is used as a tool for minimizing risk.

Topics to be discussed:

- The concept of profiling based on race
- The Oklahoma City bombing
- The Anthrax Killer
- The DC Sniper

Points to remember:

- Learn through analogy the practical flaws within racial profiling.
- There is no such thing as "suspicious" appearance, only suspicious behavior.
- False perception of knowledge is dangerous. As an example of this, let's examine public reactions to the Oklahoma City bombing of April 19, 1995.

## Question Five
### Were Muslims or Arab-Americans responsible for the Oklahoma City bombing?

In a survey based on the quiz in this book conducted in 1999 among underclassmen on the campus of a large southeastern American university, 25% of those who ranked their knowledge of Arabs, Arab-Americans, and Muslims as seven or higher on the survey based on the quiz thought Arabs were responsible for the Oklahoma City bombing. They were not! In the Oklahoma City bombing, the worst case of terrorism on US soil in American history prior to 9/11, the culprits were two young, White, Christian, former military men: Timothy McVeigh and Terry Nichols. The misperception that Muslims or Arabs committed this crime may be understandable. Muslim terrorists had attacked the World Trade Center two years earlier. Because of this, many initial news stories speculated that Islamic terrorists had staged the attack. However, the misperception this generated strongly suggests that it is not lack of knowledge that is dangerous. Rather it is the false perception of knowledge that proves dangerous and needs to be rectified.

**Suspicious Behavior, Not Suspicious Appearance**

What was the upshot of this misperception? Some media and so-called "experts" labeled the attack the work of Arab or Muslim terrorists. In the absence of concrete facts, news reports jumped to conclusions. *USA Today* headlined: "Bomb Consistent With Mideast Terror Tactics."[74] Pundits surmised that the level of horror in the act meant that Middle Easterners must be responsible because such were their traits. As a result, a backlash immediately erupted. Within the first three days, over 222 hate crimes, attacks, and incidents against Arabs and/or Muslims were reported.[75] Suhair Al Mosawi was a twenty-six-year-old Shiite Muslim and refugee from Iraq now living in Oklahoma City. The day of the bombing, a mob is said to have surrounded her home and someone threw a brick through a window. Frightened by the event, Mrs Al Mosawi, who was seven months pregnant, felt terrible pains in her abdomen, began bleeding uncontrollably, and a few hours later gave birth to a stillborn boy. A news story later reported, "His name will not be listed among the victims of the bombing."[76]

A similar situation arose after the now famed "Anthrax Killer" terrorized the mail the following month, in December 2001. The terrorist portrayed himself as a Muslim or Arab by sending messages that included such phrases as "Death to America, Allah is Great." Even so, profile authorities suspect that the responsible individual is a Christian, middle-aged, White male, with a military background. Should men fitting that description be racially profiled in post offices? No, of course not.

Experts stress that behavior, not appearance, is the effective determinant. Rafi Ron, a leading Israeli expert on aviation security, with more than thirty years of experience, was consulted by Logan Airport in Boston, Massachusetts, after September 11, 2001. His task: to improve security. When presented with the idea of profiling Arabs and Muslims, he allegedly scoffed at the thought. In November 2003, Ron and I both spoke at Northwestern University's Center for Public Safety's annual conference on racial profiling. During the question and answer session, a law enforcement officer asked Ron for an unmistakable clarification about this hypothetical situation: if he had a white guy and an Arab guy both acting in the same suspicious manner, should they each be treated in the same way? Should race not be a considered factor? Ron reiterated one of the main points of his speech: race should not matter. Instead, suspicious behavior should be the focus. If the information is driven by intelligence and a potential bad actor with specific attributes is being sought, then race, ethnicity, national origin, or religion may be incorporated, but a fishing targeting a large group based predominantly on their race, ethnicity, national origin, religion or any protected classes is simply flawed.

If the emphasis must be on what is suspicious behavior, not appearance based on one's perception of a person's race, national origin, or reli-

© 2009 Ali Farzat

gion, what exactly is that suspicious behavior? Unfortunately, it is not that simple to specify. "Suspicious" is far too often a subjective term. What may be suspicious to one person could seem completely benign to another. Is a person reading a book in a different language instantly suspicious? No. Is it suspicious to hear people speaking in a foreign language that is very unfamiliar to your ears? No. Is it suspicious to see someone praying in a way you have never seen before? No. Is it suspicious if someone looks like what we imagine a terrorist to look like? No. What if that person has a dark complexion, olive or brown skin and sports a beard or a turban? No, none of those factors alone is suspicious. This last person could simply be an observant Sikh male.

One needs to look at suspicious behavior as opposed to what one may perceive as a suspicious appearance, religion, or ethnicity. Now try these questions: Is a person wearing a ski mask inside a bank suspicious? How about a guy wearing heavy trousers in Hawaii that might conceal a gun? Maybe you get the idea. While it may be difficult to encapsulate what is suspicious, there is no such thing as a suspicious race or religion, only suspicious behavior.

Another example of failed racial profiling concerns John Allen Muhammed who perpetrated the October 2002 Beltway sniper attacks in the Washington, DC, area. The suspect's racial profile was a white, presumed Christian, former military male. While the authorities succeeded in calling out the gender, the terrorist turned out to be an African-American Muslim. Many DC area news outlets were reluctant to label him a "terrorist," as if a legitimate terrorist had to be a foreigner or linked to a particular religion. But Muhammed terrorized the community. People all over the Washington, DC, metro area stretching for hundreds of square miles were genuinely terrorized and panicked. Drivers would run from their cars into the nearest building. Others would fill gas at stations while kneeling beside their vehicles. Fear consumed many.

In combating terrorism, ultimately people need to keep two goals in mind: First, look to suspicious activity and behavior, not to appearance and ethnicity. Second, law enforcement and the government need to engage the Arab and Muslim communities both inside and outside the United States in order to build relationships and trust. A healthy, open, trusting relationship will benefit everyone. Building and maintaining *trust* is the key underlying principle. Trust is the pathway to the solution: trust from and in the community, trust from and in the government, and trust from and in law enforcement.

# Chapter Four

# Media

## From Aladdin to Saladin

THIS FOURTH CHAPTER OF THE BOOK PROBES the power of media to influence our understanding of Arabs and Muslims.

Topics to be discussed:

- The branding of Arabs and Muslims in television shows and movies.
- The media's power over and influence on our beliefs and perceptions.

Points to remember:

- Most media portrayals of Arabs and Muslims are negative.
- These portrayals tend to shape our perceptions and to provide us with incorrect and ultimately detrimental attitudes.

## Question Six

**Name one or more positive Arab *characters* in television history.**

In dealing with Questions Six and Seven, we will be taking a close look at how television and movies have portrayed Arab, Muslim, and Arab-American characters in entertainment vehicles. From time immemorial, stories have shaped perceptions of peoples and places, of great heroes and great villains, as well as characters who possess both laudable and regrettable traits. In our time, these stories come to us as movies and television shows and, because they come in a visual form, they have enormous impact on attitudes and perceptions, and deeply influence them. In a sense, they teach us our attitudes. So it is useful to analyze what they are teaching.

*© 2009 Ali Farzat*

While the following discussion has its light-hearted aspects, it's vitally important in terms of suggesting how we come to possess the attitudes we hold. While fun and interesting, these questions are also meaningful, not simply a quiz of your knowledge of Hollywood and television. Pop culture and our media are responsible for much of our education, ideas, and misperceptions about these groups. So, it is vital to address them thoroughly. I'm looking for Arab characters, specifically, as Islam is the religion and the appearance or lack thereof, may be harder to distinguish, as it is a faith. I focused my undergraduate research on the impact of media on the viewer and reader. Today, it's much more in-depth and we have social media, blogs, influencers, digital creators, and YouTubers... all of which, help shape our perceptions and misperceptions on these topics.

### Arab Characters in Television

Let's address Question Six first: Name one or more positive Arab characters in television history. The names I usually hear include: Hadji, Fez, Apu, Klinger, Danny Thomas, and Jeannie, but the number one response, by a longshot, in over twenty years of speaking on this topic is Aladdin!

Hadji was a character on the 1964 cartoon hit, *The Real Adventures of Johnny Quest*, and first appeared on the show entitled "Calcutta Adventure." He was clearly South Asian, likely Indian, perhaps even a Sikh. He wore a turban, a religious obligation for Sikh males, and his last name was *Singh*. Although, not all people named Singh are Sikhs, all Sikh males have the name Singh somewhere in their names, be it as part of their first, middle, or last name. As a show of unity, every Sikh male has Singh—which means "lion" in Punjabi. Similarly, every Sikh female has Kaur as part of her name, which means "princess" in Punjabi.

A very popular character is Fez from the comedy show, *That 70's Show*. F.E.Z. apparently stands for Foreign Exchange Z(s)tudent. According to the actor who plays Fez, Wilmer Valderamma (actually Latino, born in Miami to a Venezuelan father and Columbian mother), the character is meant to symbolize the "foreign kid," with his ethnicity remaining ambiguous. It is not clear whether he is Latino, Middle Eastern, Arab, or South Asian. Ultimately, whether he is an Arab character or not, he is still a positive character.

Apu Nahasapeemapetilon, or simply Apu to most people, is the lovable character on the cartoon *The Simpsons*. Apu, in many ways the token foreigner on the show, often brings in varied issues about being from a different culture or an outsider in our Western culture. Apu is neither an Arab nor a Muslim, but Indian. The show clearly identifies him as a follower of India's Hindu faith. Even though he is a walking stereotype, with his Quickie Mart and heavy accent, the character is actually a positive one, helping to add a certain flavor of diversity to the show.

Corporal (later Sergeant) Maxwell Q. Klinger from the 1970s hit sitcom *M\*A\*S\*H*, the famed sitcom about military medics during the Korean War, was of Lebanese descent, as was the actor portraying him, Jamie Farr. While he was a comedian who did not want to be in the war, Klinger was still a positive figure. He was not some raving lunatic with an AK-47 screaming how he was going to kill heathens for his religious beliefs. The show was a comedy and the Arab-American character was a positive one that many viewers related to and admired.

Danny Thomas, a well-known television actor-producer of some years back, was also of Lebanese descent. He was one of the first Arab-American lead characters in *Make Room for Daddy* (also known as *The Danny Thomas Show*), the hit ABC show from 1953 through 1971. Another character on the show was the lovable Uncle Tunoose, who would make references to "the old country." These characters were significant as the first to portray positive Arab-American characters leading normal and fulfilling lives as part of American society, and without any particular nexus to terrorism. I was speaking at a prestigious law firm in Washington, DC years ago, and a sweet older attorney, who happened to be Jewish, suggested Arabs and Muslims "get a sitcom... look at what Seinfeld did for us". I loved her sentiment and agreed, but told her—at the time in the early 2000's—that the climate was still so stagnant when it came to the media image that one dimensional bad guys continued to inundate the screens. [Fun point, Jerry Seinfeld, is also part Arab. His maternal grandparents were Syrian Jews born in Aleppo, Syria.] Hope brews. Back then, we had groundbreaking comedians that took the taboo and negativity and turned them on their heads, similar to what Richard Pryor did with the civil rights movement. Entertainers like Ahmed Ahmed, Maz Jobrani, Aaron Kader, Maysoon Zayid, and Dean Obeidallah have been making us laugh about the delicate topics for over two decades. Today, we have a slew of up-and-coming artists here to tell their own stories. The hit dramedy, *Ramy*, starring Ramy Youssef continues to win over audiences with its grit and wit. Most recently, in 2022, *Mo*, starring Mo Amer on Netflix received critical acclaim.

Incidentally, through his work at the American Lebanese Syrian Associated Charities (ALSAC), Danny Thomas helped start St. Jude Children's Research Hospital, now America's fourth largest charity.

Although played by a blue-eyed American blonde, Jeannie, the Genie from *I Dream of Jeannie*, the comedy that ran from 1965 through 1970, suggested that Arabs come in all shapes and sizes, with all types of appearances, facial features, and skin tones. Most people did not realize that Jeannie's character was technically Arab, supposedly born in 64 BC in Mesopotamia, which includes present-day Iraq and Syria. The term "genie" is a derivation from the Arabic word *jin-ny*, meaning spirit.

The positives are few and far in between. Another recent character is Sayid, one of the survivors on the ABC drama *LOST*. Sayid is an Iraqi, a former member of the Republican Guard under the command of Saddam Hussein. Though early in the series other characters made negative comments based on stereotypes about Arabs and Muslims, such as accusing him of being behind the plane crash, Sayid is an extremely positive character on the show. This strikes a powerful chord with the viewers as it helps to humanize someone they have perceived as the enemy. He is no longer viewed through the lens of his ethnicity or faith. More recently, Sam Hanna, played by LL Cool J, on *NCIS:*

Los Angeles is the only current Muslim main characters on television. While the character's faith could be portrayed more accurately as an opportunity for insight and understanding, I'll take what I can get. The producers are welcome to reach out and help build a realistic faith as was done with Don Cheadle's character in the spectacular thriller, *Traitor*. More on that in the film segment.

Had the question been reversed, asking for negative Arab characters in television history, there would be many from which to choose. One of the worst offenders was *JAG* on CBS. Fairly regularly, the antagonist was the ultimate negative stereotype, the "brown," scruffy, dirty Arab trying to harm the innocent, blond, American woman. In a John Wayne-ish manner, the hero of the show always swooped in to save the day.

Following 9/11, it became the fad to do shows about combating terrorism. They capitalized on people's fears (and in many instances added to levels of paranoia). Such shows rarely lasted more than a single season and included *Threat Matrix* on ABC, *The Grid* on TNT, and *The Agency*, *The Unit*, and *Navy: NCIS* on CBS. Each of those shows often had the antagonist as an Arab or Muslim.

Every so often other shows delve into the large pool of ignorance for story ideas. For example, on NBC's *The West Wing*, which was largely well-written, an early episode involved Syria shooting down an American civilian jetliner, resulting in US President Bartlet and his staff discussing carpet-bombing Damascus. In reality, Syria has never attacked the United States in any capacity. In later seasons, the writers sometimes concocted fake Arab nations to create a potential attack-defense situation.

One 2004 *West Wing* episode focused on the Abu Ghraib scandal in Iraq. Based loosely on real events, its ultimate message was that war between Islam and Christianity is brewing. Consequently "we" must heighten our awareness of Arabs and Muslims. Arab-Americans were seen as equally suspect. The episode went so far as to portray Arab-Americans en masse as assassins roaming freely in our cities. It blurred the line between fact and fiction. Having former New York City Mayor Rudy Guiliani appear as himself sent a confusing message, blurring the line between what aspects were pure entertainment and which were reality replayed. Considering the negative messaging at the time about Muslims, Arabs, and Arab-Americans, the show sent a frightening and dangerous message about a sub-community in society.

However, other shows that are usually neutral, occasionally portray positive aspects of Arabs, Arab-Americans, or Muslims. The ABC comedy *The George Lopez Show*, the first mainstream sitcom to feature a majority Latino cast, addressed a very important issue for the Arab-American community in one episode: employment discrimination. In the episode, George and others at George's small airplane plant deliberated about whether, on one hand, Hosni, an Arab-American employee, ought to be fired because he was Arab or, on the other, should be judged based on his personality and work ethic. Although Hosni lost his job, the episode broke barriers and addressed important issues. For it, the American-Arab Anti-Discrimination Committee awarded George Lopez and his show the 2003 Annual Tolerance Award.

As a summation of this section, it is worth noting just how strong an impact television makes on children, on us, and all who watch it. Our perceptions and behavior are highly influenced and shaped by what we experience through the media. Studies have shown that images in the media—especially television—can change how we think about and relate to other people. While children and adolescents are particularly likely to be influenced, none of us are immune. If we were, no one would pay to run commercials!

Having said that, it should come as no surprise that much of what we know—or believe we know—about Muslims or Arabs comes from the various forms of media, television shows, social media, both print and electronic news, films, and so on. Oftentimes, this information is skewed, one-sided, or simply focuses on the negative. We know that bad news sells, so we shouldn't be surprised that our information sources often focus on bad news. We rarely hear positive stories about Arabs or Muslims living in the United States or anywhere else in the world in any media. Consequently, it is sadly not surprising that so many people take the most recent story of a horrible bombing in Iraq or violent protest against the US embassy in Pakistan to be reflective of all Arabs or Muslims. These biases are not limited to domestic US media. International media also use the widely accepted "if it bleeds, it leads" news strategy. It is important that we recognize existing media biases in order to better decipher fact from fiction or exaggeration, and to understand that stereotyping entire communities of people based on the publicized actions of a few is incorrect.

## Question Seven

**Name one or more positive Arab characters in movie history.**

Although not a movie *character*, many respondents—mostly women—name Omar Sharif, a Lebanese-Egyptian who grew up in Egypt to become a successful actor in the Arab film world before crossing over to Hollywood. There, Sharif played a number of memorable characters including the title role in *Dr. Zhivago*, Nicky Arnstein opposite Barbra Streisand in *Funny Girl*, as well as Sherif Ali ibn el Kharish in *Lawrence of Arabia*. (Curiously, Alec Guinness, an Englishman, and Anthony Quinn, a Mexican-American, also played prominent Arab characters in the latter film.)

### Arab Characters in Movie History

The usual responses include: characters from *Aladdin*, *The Siege*, *The Mummy* series, *The Scorpion King*, *Hidalgo*, "the guy with the fez in Indiana Jones," *Robin Hood: Prince of Thieves*, and *Lawrence of Arabia*.

Disney's *Aladdin* is by far the most common response, often given with almost childlike enthusiasm. For that reason, it may be worthwhile to examine *Aladdin* in some detail to show how media prejudice works. Released in 1992, *Aladdin* proved to be a blockbuster hit and winner of two Academy Awards. Aladdin was portrayed as the brave peasant hero who rids the empire of the evil Jafar. On the surface, this movie is an innocent children's cartoon with good triumphing over evil. When put under a magnifying glass, however, it turns out to carry a freight of negative stereotypes.

Interestingly, the movie received criticism for its depictions of Arabs. In a *Des Moines Register* editorial, for example, Professor Joanne Brown of Drake University stated that *Aladdin*'s villains displayed "dark-hooded eyes and large hooked noses...perhaps I am sensitive to this business of noses because I am Jewish." She noted how distressed she would be if Disney created a feature-length cartoon, portraying folk-tale Jews as Shylock, the miserly Jewish money-lender in Shakespeare's *Merchant of Venice*.[77]

*Aladdin* also featured songs that were full of blatant bigotry. For example, the opening song included these lyrics: "Oh, I come from a land, from a faraway place, where the caravan camels roam, where they cut off your ear, if they don't like your face, it's barbaric, but hey, it's home."[78]

As with most cartoons, the character of Aladdin was modeled on a real person. Think about it, how close does Dory look to Ellen?: Tom Cruise was the inspiration for Aladdin. Since Arabs come in all colors and shapes, it's possible for an Arab Aladdin to resemble Cruise. However, the protagonists Aladdin and Jasmine were fair-skinned, had good posture, "normal" noses, and spoke perfect American English. By contrast, villains and buffoon bystanders had brown complexions, large, droopy eyes, beards, and big, crooked noses and backs. Their English was heavily accented. On a not so subtle level, the film reinforced that if they look and sound like "us", they were the good guys and if they look and sound different, well then.... In addition, throughout *Aladdin*, Arab culture was belittled. Arabic names were mispronounced and Arabic street signs were rendered as meaningless gibberish and squiggles.[79]

Two years later, Disney released a successful direct-to-video item, *The Return of Jafar*, a sequel to *Aladdin*. Following reactions to *Aladdin*, Disney instituted a "policy of prior consultation," promising that films representing minority cultures would be reviewed and critiqued prior to postproduction. However, neither the American-Arab Anti-Discrimination Committee nor any other Arab-American organization reviewed the sequel. As before, bigotry and negative stereotypes filled *The Return of Jafar*. This time the public sent numerous letters criticizing Disney.

The pressure had some effect. In 1996, when Disney released the third movie in the series, *Aladdin and the King of Thieves*, producers consulted with experts and the Arab-American community and made positive changes. Aladdin and Jasmine had darker complexions than in the first two films and the accents of the characters were addressed. Moreover, neutral bystander characters were shown as good human beings.[80]

The 2019 live action Aladdin almost made up for the past. Disney did their best with diversity. Will Smith was manic enough to make Robin Williams proud. Aladdin was played by Egyptian-Canadian, Mena Massoud – though initially there were rumors that Dev Patel would be cast. Patel is of Indian extraction. Fortunately, Disney recognized that not all brown people are the same and cast an actual Arab to play the Arab title role. Naomi Scott, of Indian-English extraction was cast as Jasmine. The cast was full of a broad range of diverse ethnic backgrounds, skin tones, and accents.

*The Siege* (1998) starring Denzel Washington, Bruce Willis, Annette Bening, and Tony Shalhoub opens with a terrible bombing in New York City. The imposition of martial law results. Arabs, Arab-Americans, and Muslims are soon rounded up and placed in makeshift camps in sports stadiums. The film vilifies Arab immigrants, US citizens of Arab descent, and Muslims, and throughout it anti-Arab voiceovers are present. At its core it proposes that most, if not all, Arabs, Arab-Americans, and Muslims are terrorists and should be treated with grave suspicion. Before the detonation of a super-bomb, director Edward Zwick shows terrorists going through the Islamic pre-prayer holy cleansing process, creating a direct—but wholly false—link between the Islamic prayer process in Islam and terrorism. Unfortunately, Zwick ignored recommendations from Arab and Muslim experts. Tony Shalhoub's portrayal of an Arab-American FBI agent was the one positive Arab-American character in the movie. However, as Professor Jack Shaheen notes in his book, *Reel Bad Arabs*: "Though Shalhoub's character is a good one, it can never offset all those scenes that show Arab Muslims murdering men, women, and children."

The *Washington Post*'s Sharon Waxman makes a valid point through analogy: a nefarious rabbi exhorts his extremist, ultra-Orthodox followers to plant bombs against Arab sympathizers in America. Innocents are killed and maimed. The FBI starts rounding up Orthodox Jews and putting them in camps. Or how about this: a Catholic priest has molested an altar boy. The church refuses to hand him and other offenders over to police. The FBI starts rounding up clerics in an attempt to ferret them out. These provocative story lines—unlikely, perhaps, but not entirely implausible—would certainly spark an outcry from Jewish and Catholic interest groups. The question is: Would Hollywood choose to portray them in the first place?[81]

The positive aspect of *The Siege* juxtaposes a general who uses force and coercion, shooting first and asking questions later, against a coolheaded FBI agent who wants to engage Arabs and Muslims. Ultimately level-headed and inclusive thinking triumphs. The angry general is arrested for crimes against humanity, for torturing and killing a suspect.

In general, *The Mummy* series—*The Mummy* (1999), *The Mummy Returns* (2001), and the prequel, *The Scorpion King* (2002)—is demeaning to Arabs, specifically Egyptians. *The Mummy*, filled with bumbling, dirty, evil Arabs, has been called a "masterpiece of bigotry."[82] The movie faces off slimy and filthy towel-heads against handsome, noble-looking Englishmen and Americans. *The Mummy Returns* was just as bad except for Israeli-born actor Oded Fehr's characterization of Ardeth Bey, an heroic Bedouin.

*The Scorpion King*, on the other hand, is a bit more positive in its portrayals. The movie depicts the rise of the leader known as the Scorpion King in pre-Pharaonic Egypt, well before the Arab emergence. Still, the film's comic relief, a sidekick character named Arpid, says *shukran* ("thank you," in Arabic) and *la*, which means "no."

> FYI—The Real Scorpion King
> *Although the movie was not meant to be a true story, evidence exists that the king who first united the tribes and ruled ancient Egypt was known as King Scorpion.*

Again, the public knowledge, the role media plays, confuses and conflates. In conducting research on Arab or Muslim characters I kept seeing the two intertwined. Whether it was an NPR article in 2022 that was positively trying to highlight the lack of Muslim representation in media. "Muslims make up 25% of the global population and Islam is the fastest-growing religion in the world-but Muslims only comprise 1% of characters shown on popular television series in the U.S., U.K., Australia, and New Zealand." At the same time, the photo of the person of color for the story was that of Archie Panjabi, a non-Muslim, British actress of Indian extraction. Another article discussing "Five Hollywood Movies with Arab Lead Actors" gets it wrong with at least two. One is Kumail Nanjiani (from *The Big Sick* and *Eternals*) who, while from a Muslim family, is of Pakistani origin and thus not Arab and the other is Ana Lily Amirpour who is of Iranian origin or "Persian, like a cat", as Maz Jobrani would say, but again, even those trying to shed more light on the topic, often get it wrong.

Here are some other movies worth noting: The 1962 Oscar winning classic *Lawrence of Arabia*—with Peter O'Toole as the title character, Alec Guinness as Prince Faisal, Anthony Quinn as Auda Abu Tayi, and Omar Sharif as Sherif Ali Ibn El Kharish—may have been plagued with historical misinformation. It suggested that Lawrence "saved" the Arabs during World War I. (Arabs tend to regard Lawrence's crucial contribution as being his ability to supply them arms and equipment.) But the movie's portrayal of Arabs showed them demonstrating honor, valor, courage, and hospitality. Moreover, the Hollywood stars of the day were all playing Arabs. Imagine, if you will, the stars of *Ocean's 11*—George Clooney, Brad Pitt, and Matt Damon—all playing Arab characters in an upcoming movie, and they win Oscars for it. It's unlikely that would happen today, but it did in 1962.

***Hidalgo*** (2004) featured Arab characters ranging from positive to neutral to negative. Omar Sharif played a patriarch sheik who fights in the name of love and honor.

***Zero Dark Thirty*** (2012) focusing on the manhunt for Osama bin Laden and while fiction is loosely based on reality, including real life characters. Most notably, is "Roger", the CIA counterterrorism chief who is a White convert to Islam, as we see him pray inside his office at Langley. Incredibly powerful and real.

***Syriana*** (2005)—a powerful thriller revolving around the life of a CIA undercover officer, Arab and American politicians, power brokers, and the roots of terrorism—explored high-level politics and corruption between the Arab World and the United States. It offered fair portrayals, with George Clooney in an Oscar-winning role, bad Arabs and good Arabs, and everyone in between. In my opinion, this film does a great job looking into how a terrorist is created and managed.

***Robin Hood: Prince of Thieves*** (1991) features Morgan Freeman playing a Saracen warrior—"Azeem"—indebted to Robin Hood for saving his life. Wearing appropriate garb, carrying a scimitar (the weapon of choice for Arab warriors at the time), the character displays honor, courage, strength, valor, respect, and humility, and prays as a Muslim. The movie alludes to the superior technology of the Arab World at that time. Robin Hood looks through the telescope and is puzzled by how close the advancing soldiers appear. The more recent 2017 iteration cast Jamie Foxx as "Yahya" – and while not as awesome as Morgan Freeman's character, it is a positive one, nonetheless.

FYI—Salah-el-Din (Saladin) 1138—1193
*Salah-el-Din (literally Righteousness of Faith) was born to a Kurdish family in present-day Tikrit, Iraq. Known as a great*

*military leader, he led the Muslim resistance to the European Crusaders, eventually recapturing Palestine from the Crusader Kingdom of Jerusalem. At the height of his power, he ruled over Egypt, Syria, Iraq, and most of the Arabian Peninsula. Notable beyond his military skills were his chivalry and honor. Whenever he had the upper hand in a battle, he would accept a peaceful and just surrender. He would offer enemies a chance to live among Muslims in peace or pay a tax and earn their freedom. He strove for peace with the Crusaders and had high respect for his opponents. At one point Salah-el-Din sent his personal physicians to aid the English King Richard the Lionheart, when he fell ill. Although Salah-el-Din gained riches from his victories, when his treasury was opened after his death, there was too little money to pay for his funeral. This was because Salah-el-Din had throughout his life given his wealth to the poor and needy. His tomb lies in Damascus and is a major tourist attraction.*

***The 13th Warrior*** (1999) told the story of Ahmed Ibn Fahdlan (Antonio Banderas) and is based on the historical records of the real-life Ibn Fahdlan, who kept detailed accounts of his endeavors with Norse warriors. The character, full of honor, courage, and humility, wears the traditional garb of the time, alters the large Viking sword into a scimitar, and prays as a Muslim.

***Kingdom of Heaven*** (2005) by far the best movie of its generation in its portrayals of Arabs, Muslims, and Salah-el-Din (Saladin), showed how the twelfth century Crusades, like most great wars in history, may have had religion as the justification, but ultimately were about power and land. Loosely based on the life of Balian of Ibelin (Orlando Bloom), the movie also focused on the internal struggles for peace or war within the hearts of the Christian Europeans, and the valor and honor of their noble enemy, Salah-el-Din (Ghassan Massoud), who ruled out of Damascus and is buried there. The movie portrayed the Arabs and Muslims of the time as the more advanced, humble leaders who are better organized than their European counterparts. I had the opportunity to work with Ridley Scott's people when we first got a copy of the script, which was initially plagued with concerns. The studio representatives were certain and confident of the final product and invited a number of us to a private screening of the film before it was released. The final product was incredible, accurate, and positive. When we asked what changed, they said, they hired real Arabs and Muslims to play those parts and they taught them about history from their side. Fantastic!

*Traitor* (2008) is another movie that took great steps forward in its portrayals of Islam. Writer/Director Jeffrey Nachmanoff aimed for accuracy and reality with this complicated tale about terrorism. Samir Horn, spectacularly played by Don Cheadle, is a former US Special Forces soldier caught in a complex web of good and evil and driven by his faith in God. Horn is an Arab-American and devout Muslim (born in Sudan to a Sudanese father and African-American mother). The movie, unlike anything before it, takes an honest look at terrorism and Islam without vilifying the faith. I was fortunate enough to consult with Nachmanoff and two producers, Anjalika Mathur Nigam and Jeff Silver as they sought an accurate portrayal of the protagonist Arab-American Muslim and am quite pleased with the overall storyline and its execution.

*Batman Begins* (2005) has a nexus to the topic. To quote Batman himself, "I'm Batman". I'm constantly hungering to learn more about these things that interest me, inspire me, and define me. In my research, I discovered that Batman's initial coach and leader of the League of Shadows is Ra's al Ghul. His name is Arabic for "The head of the demon/ghoul" (another Arabic word). The villain debuted in the Batman comics in 1971. While Liam Neeson does a wonderful portrayal, it would have been refreshing to have an Arab play the cool villain. That would at least be better off than the constant one-dimensional villains we often see portrayed. The so-called Whitewashing in Hollywood is fairly common. As of this writing, Leonardo DiCaprio is set to play the Muslim Persian poet Jalal Al-Din Muhammad Rumi, or Rumi, for short. His faith is often side-stepped, yet his poetry and philosophy are everywhere.

In *Reel Bad Arabs*, which was the primary resource for this chapter of the book, Jack Shaheen reviewed more than nine hundred films. He broke film portrayals into several categories, among them was what he deemed a "Best List." How many films do you think he assigned to that list? Only twelve. Let that sink in. Shaheen considers that offerings on the television front are not much better.

Shaheen ends with a poignant suggestion, "Writers and producers ought to show us as true Americans: devout fathers and mothers, military veterans, teens catching flyballs, and families walking on the beach. Show us as we are."[83] I often recall Patrick Stewart's Professor Charles Xavier speaking in the first X-Men film and the one phrase that stayed with me as an American who happens to be Muslim, who happens to be of Arab origin was: "We're not what you think." Not that any of us have Adamantium in our bodies or can read minds (or can we?), but that fear of the unknown, the fear of that which we perceive as different has always resonated. One could replace the word Mutant with Muslim or Arab or Black or Jewish and the sentence would ring true for so many. It should come as no surprise that the X-Men comics were at least partially inspired by the civil rights movement. The color blue equates a different person of color. Magneto vs. Professor X are who else than Malcom X and Martin Luther King, Jr. I know, blew my mind as well!

As was demonstrated, had Question Seven asked for any *negative* characters, we could have easily found such examples. I flippantly mention qualifiers such as a number of Chuck Norris movies, from *Invasion USA* to *The President's Man* and *The President's Man 2: Line in the Sand* (formerly *The President's Man 2: Holy War*) to *Delta Force, Operation Delta Force 2*, and *Delta Force 3*. Although Norris did not appear in *Operation Delta Force 2* and *Delta Force 3*, he did do *Delta Force 2*, where the bad guys were Columbian drug lords. But not to worry, *Operation Delta Force 2* and *Delta Force 3* still had the villainous Arabs. Chuck Norris just happened not to star in them. I mean, I love the guy too, but could he have sprinkled just a bit of all that ass-kicking to another demographic? Arnold Schwarzenegger's movie *True Lies* was horrible in its portrayals and messaging—the villain again being the negative stereotypical Muslim Arab with curly black hair, big nose, and scruffy dirty beard. *Rules of Engagement* not only vilifies and attacks an entire existing Arab country (Yemen), but also denigrates a cross-section of that society, as we see women, children, and the like all ultimately guilty of unbelievable violence and terror. I'm a child of the 80's. I remember one of my favorite, dare I say, inspiring films as a child was Iron Eagle. Yes, that 1986 classic starring the magnificent Louis Gosset Jr. and Jason Gedrick. It was a sobering moment for me, when one day watching it for the sixty-something time as a kid, I realized – in typical 80's diversity – there were the White, Black, and female protagonists included and all of a sudden, it hit me that I looked more like the bad guys. That's a hard pill to swallow for an eleven-year-old.

This exercise demonstrates that all groups, all faiths, all ethnicities tend to be stereotyped by television programs and movies. For most groups, however, there are positive portrayals. But when it comes to Arabs and Muslims, it is very hard to find the positive side of the coin. That's why it's important to recognize that our popular culture not only dominates globally, but also makes an impact on each and every one of us, shaping our beliefs and perceptions. We could stand to tell better and more accurate stories. I would seriously love to produce Andalusia: Dawn of Greatness or bring to life the only Muslim Arab-American superhero Simon Baz, aka Green Lantern—no disrespect to Ryan Reynolds, but I promise to do a better job than his Hal Jordan Green Lantern iteration. We need to coordinate and collaborate across ideology, faith, national origin and more and just work towards the overall good. In fact, that's not enough, good isn't good enough anymore. We have to work towards the overall Best! I have said for years it's up to the good people on all sides to counter the fear, ignorance, and hate, also on all sides.

# Chapter Five

# Arabs & Arab-Americans

## Not as close as one would think.

THIS FIFTH CHAPTER OF THE BOOK EXPLORES the history of majority - minority interaction and looks at the distinction between Arab-Americans and Arabs beyond US borders.

Topics to be discussed:

- Labeling others and historical maltreatment of minorities
- Arabs vs. Arab-Americans
- Negative stereotypes in our society

Points to remember:

- Profiling based on one's race is ineffective and counterproductive.
- The dangers of self-perceived knowledge.
- All Americans—hyphenated or not—are Americans.
- Arabs and Arab-Americans are not the first, nor will they be the last, groups to be targeted within our society.

## Question Eight

**Were Arab-Americans responsible for the 9/11 attacks on our country?**
Even today, years after the September 11, 2001, attacks, people still answer this question as true. It is false.

### Arabs or Arab-Americans?

This book has already addressed the differences between Arabs and Muslims, now it's time to distinguish between Arabs and Arab-Americans.

Arab-American is a hyphenated term. The word "Arab" defines what type of Americans they are. If assimilation were total, we would not still be using hyphenated terms in our society. But we have not reached that point. We still define each other—and ourselves. African vs. African-American, Asian vs. Asian-American, Anglo vs. Anglo-American, Arab vs. Arab-American… ideally we shed the hyphenation, hold hands, and sing kumbaya, but it's not that simple yet.

None of the 9/11 terrorists were Arab-American. All were Arab non-immigrant visitors to the United States. Not immigrants, who were trying to become US citizens. They did not have green cards. They were here on student visas, visitor visas, or employment visas.

Did US citizens provide material support for the 9/11 terrorists in the form of hosting, logistical support, and so forth? The investigation never clearly stated whether these men acted alone or with support from others. If they did in fact get support from others, we still do not know if that support came from Arab-Americans. Mind you, someone like me does not recognize them as Muslim any more than you may identify the KKK as Christian. They were certainly not the same religion as mine.

An important point of clarification may be useful. Generally speaking, and as discussed earlier, hospitality is common and traditional within Muslim and Arab culture. Some or all of the 9/11 terrorists may have requested aid when they first arrived in the United States. They may have asked to stay a few nights at the home of relatives (close or distant) or of friends (or friends of friends). They may have sought assistance with basic needs. If this happened, unaware of the terrorists' plans, Muslims or Arab-Americans would have willingly helped anyone to whom they had a connection. Unfortunately, if this did in fact take place, the terrorists took advantage of a cultural characteristic they knew they could manipulate.

## Question Nine
### Do you believe a negative stereotype about Muslims or Arab-Americans exists in the United States?

Do negative stereotypes about Muslims or Arab-Americans exist in the United States? Absolutely. Do negative stereotypes also exist against Arabs? Yes. What about Muslims? Also yes. Are Arab-Americans, Arabs, and Muslims the only groups facing problems due to negative stereotypes? Of course not.

**Do *You* Face a Stereotype?**

Are Arabs, Arab-Americans, and Muslims the first groups to face negative stereotypes in our society? No! Will they be the last such groups? Unfortunately no.

Since the time of the early settlers, America has been plagued by a deep strain of nativism, "the practice or policy of favoring native-born citizens as against immigrants." This has led to discrimination, first against what are now termed Native Americans, then against African-Americans, Irish, Italians, Jews, Catholics, Chinese, and Japanese. The most recent groups targeted for discrimination are Latino immigrants, as well as any of the so-called post 9/11 groups, Arabs, Persians, Sikhs, South Asians, Muslims, and Arab-Americans following the 9/11 attacks.

Moreover, since its emergence as a pre-eminent world power after World War I, America has also exhibited a seeming need always to envision an enemy lurking just over the horizon. After German Nazism came Soviet communism. Once the Soviet empire collapsed, a "new world order" was hailed, only to be erased by fears of Japanese economic might, the rise of modern China, Latino immigration, and then what some of the American chattering classes have decided to term "Islamo-fascism," which as mentioned previously, is an inaccurate, improper term to refer to a violent extremist movement to which some Muslims subscribe.

Let's briefly examine this pattern of discrimination. Native Americans were seen as obstacles to the fulfillment of "Manifest Destiny," a nineteenth century notion that American settlers should expand across the continent. Native Americans were commonly regarded as savages back then, fit to have their land expropriated and be herded into reservations, their way of life destroyed. "Kill the Indian, save the man" was at least one method of forced assimilation. White-skinned Christian immigrant groups—Irish, Italians, and the Swedish (in the upper Midwest)—faced discrimination because of their differentness. Majority Protestants felt strong prejudice against Catholics. American anti-Semitism dates back to the colonial era. Jews faced exclusion from businesses, universities, and social clubs until well after World War II, even today, Department of Justice reports confirm that anti-Semitic hate crimes are among the highest. Alarmed by the bugaboo of a "Yellow Peril," Congress enacted the Chinese Exclusion Act in 1882, initially only as a ten-year ban. Extended indefinitely in 1902, it was repealed only in 1943 when China was needed as an ally against Japan in World War II. Following the Pearl Harbor attack, 120,000 Japanese and Japanese-Americans were interned as a knee-jerk reaction to the attack, and because of fears that Japanese immigrants would aid a Japanese invasion of the West Coast of the United States. More recently, nativist feeling has been directed against immigrants, especially undocumented migrants, crossing the border from Mexico. Suspicions have also been aroused against Arabs, Muslims, and Arab-Americans. With the rise of Covid-19, we saw an unimaginable spike in hatred, discrimination and blame against Asians and Asian-Americans.

Among the greatest sufferers of American prejudice have been African-Americans, many of whom had ancestors brought from Africa to America as slaves. The original American Constitution counted a slave as three-fifths of a person. The civil rights struggles of the past are well known. Although much progress has been made, racial discrimination still exists. Ask a young Black man how he feels walking down the street in a predominantly white neighborhood. We continue to see fear and aggression against African-Americans, from George Floyd to Ahmaud Arbery to Breonna Taylor. I used to teach at the Washington, DC Metro Police Department—in fact, I taught the entire police force over two years. The force overwhelmingly mirrors the community which it serves and thus was majority African-American. I remember one day an officer who had been engaged in class walked up to me afterwards. He was huge, about 8 feet tall, as I looked up at him towering and smiling, he very stoically and sarcastically said, "welcome to the club," as he nodded upward. I laughed and said, "thanks, but no thanks, this club is terrible and the card is accepted anywhere!" We both laughed, but he was lightheartedly implying an added link between his community and mine, though I must say, the Arab and Muslim communities have not endured but a small percentage of what their African-American brethren have faced.

In a March 2021 Pew Research survey, 78% of Americans surveyed believed Muslims faced at least "some" discrimination. Unsurprisingly, in a series of Pew surveys from 2014 through 2019, ranking religions, Islam was consistently at the bottom (along with atheism).[84] Moreover, in its 2009 Annual Religion and Public Life Survey, the Pew Forum noted that 58% of Americans believe that Muslims face a lot of discrimination, second only to homosexuals (64%). As for violence, an alarming 38% believe that Islam encourages violence more than other religions, whereas only 45% believe Islam is no more likely than other faiths to encourage violence.

Pew also confirms that people who know a Muslim are less likely to see Islam as violent. Apparently too few people know a Muslim, since 45% of Americans see Islam as "different" than their own belief. Even Pew errs in stating, ". . . the Muslim name for God is Allah." As we mentioned earlier, "Allah" is merely the Arabic term for God. Arab Christians and Arab Jews both call God, "Allah."

Although plagued by many forms of discrimination based on power, wealth, education, family status, and even religion, the Arab World does not have overt discrimination based on race. Of course, there exist different forms of individual bigotry, but on a societal level racial prejudice is much less prevalent.

In sum, Arabs, Arab-Americans, and Muslims are not the first groups, nor will they be the last, to be stigmatized and stereotyped in our nation. Unless we learn how to get over our fear of one another, however, we will never quite learn how to deal with and embrace one another's differences.

Overcoming ignorance is the key. To quote Yoda, the Jedi master from George Lucas' *Star Wars*: "Ignorance leads to fear . . . fear leads to anger . . . anger leads to hate . . . hate leads to suffering."[85] This quotation paraphrases Supreme Court Justice Louis D. Brandeis from 1927. "But they knew that . . . fear breeds repression; that repression breeds hate; that hate menaces stable government; that the path of safety lies in the opportunity to discuss freely supposed grievances and proposed remedies; and that the fitting remedy for evil counsels is good ones."[86]

# Chapter Six

# Who's Who in Muslim and Arab-America

## From the heart pump to the ice cream cone.

THIS SIXTH CHAPTER OF THE BOOK LOOKS at the civic and cultural contributions of both Muslims and Arab-Americans to American society.

Topics to be discussed:

- Famous Muslim and Arab-Americans
- Contributions made to different parts of society by Muslim and Arab-Americans

Points to remember:

- Muslims and Arab-Americans have played a role in every segment of our society.
- Most people know Muslims or Arab-Americans in their community, but may not realize it.
- Americans of Arab descent or of the Islamic faith are as "American" as everyone else.
- Lebanon is the country of origin of the highest number of Arab-Americans in the United States.

## Question Ten

**Circle any Arab-American public figures in the following categories.**
Before examining Question Ten, here's a related one. Can you think of any famous or influential Muslim and/or Arab-Americans? (Don't

consider those already discussed.) Because image and perception shape attitudes, it is important to recognize Muslim and Arab-American individuals making positive contributions in our society.

Here are some notable Arab-Americans and Western Muslims:

Anees—rising Hip-hop/rap artist.

Joseph Abboud—famous fashion designer.

General John Abizaid—former commander of the US Central Command.

Mohammed Abu-Ghazaleh—CEO and Chairman of Del Monte Produce.

F. Murray Abraham—Oscar winner, Best Actor for *Amadeus*, 1985.

Spencer Abraham—former US Senator from Michigan, US Secretary of Energy.

Ahmed Ahmed—Egyptian American comedian (*Axis of Evil*).

Riz Ahmed—Oscar winning actor of Pakistani origin. First Muslim to be nominated for Best Actor, *The Sound of Metal*, 2021. He won in 2022 for *The Long Goodbye*.

Mahershala Ali—Oscar winner Muslim convert. First Muslim Actor to win an Oscar. *Moonlight*, 2017.

Paul Anka—legendary musician and lyricist.

Yasmine Bleeth—motion picture and television actress.

Don Bustany—legendary radio personality and co-founder of several radio shows, including Top 40.

Cherien Dabis—rising star in acting and directing. Emmy nominated for her work.

Dr. Michael DeBakey—Houston-based pioneer surgeon, inventor of the heart pump.

Yamila Diaz-Rahi—international model, *Sports Illustrated* cover girl.

Emelio Estefan—singer Gloria's husband/manager, of Cuban Arab descent.

Robert George—White House Santa for seven administrations.

Khalil Gibran—great twentieth century Arab-American poet/philosopher, died 1931.

Bella Hadid—supermodel of Arab and Dutch extraction.

Sammy Hagar—former lead singer of Van Halen.

Joseph Haggar—founder, Haggar clothing, largest manufacturer of men's slacks.

Najeeb Halaby—former head of Federal Aviation Administration and CEO of Pan-American Airlines, died 2003. His daughter Lisa married Jordan's King Hussein, taking the name Queen Noor.

Tony Ismail—president and founder of Alamo Flags, largest US flag retailer.

Janet Jackson—converted to Islam in 2012

Assad Jebara—businessman and designer of Zana-di Jeans.

James Jebara—first jet ace.

Steve Jobs—Co-Founder of Apple, Inc. is the son of two grad students, an American mother, and a Syrian Father, Abdulfattah John Jandali.

Maz Jobrani—Iranian-American comedic genius.

Aaron Kader—Palestinian/Mormon comedian (*Axis of Evil*).

Casey Kasem—the voice of numerous cartoon voices, including some in *Scooby Doo* and *Batman & Robin*, as well as co-founder and host of *Casey's Top 40*.

DJ Khaled—record executive, rap star, and producer.

Fazlur Rahman Khan—the "Einstein of structural engineering"—he revolutionized how skyscrapers are built.

Candice Lightner—founder of Mothers Against Drunk Driving (MADD).

Rami Malek—brought Freddie Mercury to life and earned his Best Actor Oscar.

Ed Masry—lead lawyer in the Erin Brockovich case.

Christa McAuliffe—notable teacher, victim of NASA space shuttle *Challenger* tragedy.

Wentworth Miller—rising actor, star of Fox's *Prison Break*.

George Mitchell—former US Senator from Maine, former senate majority leader, chairman of Disney Board of Directors, negotiator of Irish peace agreement, investigator of steroid use in baseball.

Ibtihaj Muhammad—first female Muslim-American athlete to earn a medal at the Olympics.

Bampett Muhammad—Revolutionary War hero who served under General George Washington.

Kathy Najimy—comedian/actress.

Jacques Nasser—former CEO of Ford Motor Company.

Dean Obeidallah—Palestinian/Sicilian comedian (*Axis of Evil*) and radio personality.

Bobby Rahal—Indy 500 race car champion.

Nick Rahall II—Congressman from West Virginia.

Diane Rehm—Nationally syndicated radio personality.

Boris Said—multitalented professional race car driver.

Point to Ponder
The Origin of the Ice Cream Cone
*At the 1904 St. Louis World's Fair, there were fifty ice cream booths, all of them serving ice cream in glass dishes. Next to one of these worked a pastry maker, Ernest Hamwi, who had emigrated from Syria in 1903. Mr. Hamwi was selling zalabia, a crisp, wafer-like pastry baked on a flat waffle-iron and served thin, sprinkled with sugar. This waffle was popular throughout the*

*Arab World as well as in France and Scandinavia, known as rosenkuken in Germany, gaufre in Belgium.*

*The ice cream booth next to Mr. Hamwi ran out of clean dishes. To be of help, he quickly rolled one of his warm wafer waffles into the shape of a cone. As it cooled, the wafer set in the shape of a cone. When the vendor placed ice cream in it, the ice cream cone was born. Soon it was on its way to becoming a great American institution.*[87]

Lucie Salhany—first woman to head a TV network (Fox).

Tom Shadyac—film director (*Ace Ventura, Nutty Professor*, and *Liar, Liar*) .

George Shaheen—founder of Accenture (formerly Anderson Consulting).

Jack Shaheen—Author, professor, and subject matter expert on Arab portrayal in the media.

Donna Shalala—first Arab-American to hold a cabinet post, longest-ever serving Secretary of Health and Human Services, former President of New York's Hunter College, former Chancellor of the University of Wisconsin, present President of the University of Miami.

John E. Sununu—former US Senator from New Hampshire.

Chris Sununu—governor of New Hampshire.

John H. Sununu—former White House Chief of Staff, former Governor of New Hampshire, father of the present New Hampshire Governor.

Vic Tayback—Mel on the sitcom *Alice*.

Danny Thomas—former actor, comedian, and founder of St. Jude Children's Hospital.

Helen Thomas—former president of the Gridiron Club.

Frank Zappa—father of alternative music.

Ahmed Zewail—won the Nobel prize for Chemistry.

NFL legends Don Shula and John Elway are also part Arab. Robert Saleh, is the first Muslim and Arab NFL head coach thanks to the New York Jets.

Finally, perhaps most importantly, Ernest Hamwi, the inventor of the ice cream cone, an Arab-American of Syrian decent. Where would the world be without the ice cream cone?

Now let's address the correct answers to Question Ten: Circle Arab-American public figures in various categories. Again, we are looking at ethnicity vs. religion here. There are countless examples of Muslim Americans from physicians to leaders, from comedians to athletes, some of whom we highlighted above.

### Arab-American Contributions to American Life

The list of names includes public figures who hail from Central and South America.

While some three million people of Arab descent live in the United States, in North, Central, and South America as a whole there are closer to ten to thirty million Arabs. They are more fully integrated into their societies than their cousins in the US. They are comparable to Italian and Irish communities in the US who long ago became part of the proverbial melting pot.

Of these pop stars, who is the Arab-American: Shakira, Christina Aguilera, or Britney Spears? The correct answer is Shakira, who is half Columbian, half Lebanese. "Shakira," is derived from the Arabic term "shuker," which means gratitude. Shakira's two heritages coexist. She is proud of both. On her first English language CD *Laundry Service*, she sings in English, Spanish, as well as Arabic (which may explain why you may not understand all of the songs!). In some of her music videos she also belly dances, an Arab style of dancing. Most recently, when she played the Superbowl halftime show in 2020, she leaned into the camera and did the Arabic celebratory sound known as ululating (check out the FYI box below), but my social media blew up with people inquiring why Shakira was doing a turkey-call on live television!

Who is the Arab-American former presidential candidate: consumer advocate Ralph Nader, Former Vice President Al Gore, Senator Mitt Romney? The answer is Ralph Nader, who is of Lebanese descent. His role in enacting seatbelt laws saved many lives and made an impact on all Americans. His mother, Rose Nader, authored a Middle Eastern cookbook, *It Happened in the Kitchen*, which included wise sayings of Ralph's father, Nathra Nader.

Who is the Arab-American movie starlet: Salma Hayek, star of such films as *From Dusk 'til Dawn*, *Desperado*, and *Frida* (which she produced and for which she was nominated for an Academy Award); Shannon Elizabeth, most famous as the exchange student in the *American Pie* movies; or Denise Richards, Bond girl in *The World is Not Enough* and *Wild Things*? Remember, there is at least one Arab-American in each category; in some instances there are two. In this question two out of three of your choices are Arab-American, so your chances were relatively high to get one right. The correct answers are Hayek and Elizabeth. Hayek (both her first and last names are Arabic) is half Lebanese and half Mexican. Elizabeth was born in Texas but is of Syrian descent through her father's side.

Who is the Arab-American 1980s pop star (you may think this is easy, but it could be a trick question): Debbie Gibson, teen queen most famous for her hit single "Only In My Dreams"; Paula Abdul, music video dancer/choreographer, recently in the spotlight again through her appearances as a judge on the television show *American Idol*, and famous for such hits as "Cold Hearted Snake," "Straight Up," and "Forever Your Girl"; or Tiffany, most famous for touring malls throughout the United States in order to reach the public with her music? Again, there are two correct answers: Paula Abdul and Tiffany. Paula Abdul (Abdul is an Arabic name) is half Syrian-Jewish/half Canadian. Born in Oklahoma, Tiffany is of Syrian descent. She was named Tiffany Renée Darwish (Darwish is an Arabic name). She's credited with discovering New Kids on The Block; they opened for her in 1987!

Point to Ponder
Arab Jews

*People sometimes find it confusing that someone like Paula Abdul can be of both Syrian and Jewish descent. Here's how. Damascus, Syria's capital, is one of the oldest cities in the world, perhaps the world's oldest continuously inhabited city. Its archeological sites date back to 6000 BC. Jews have lived in Damascus since ancient times. Some still live there—and in other Arab countries.*

*Other famous Jews of Arab origin include Max Azria, the fashion designer and founder of BCBG, who is originally from Tunisia; Paul Marciano, co-founder of GUESS, who is of Moroccan descent; famed fashion designer Isaac Mizrahi of Syrian ancestry;*

*and American Idol sensation, Elliot Yamin, the son of an Iraqi Jewish father. Last but certainly not least, Jerry Seinfeld, famed comedian and American pop culture figure, is the son of a Hungarian father and a Syrian mother. Who knew?![88]*

Who is the Arab-American NFL quarterback: Doug Flutie, Jeff George, or Drew Brees? Here again, we have two correct answers. Doug Flutie is most famous for the miracle Hail Mary at Boston College in 1984, which clinched the Heisman Trophy for him. Of Syrian-Lebanese descent, Flutie has also led the Buffalo Bills and the San Diego Chargers in the NFL. Jeff George, also of Lebanese descent, has played with the Washington Redskins, Atlanta Falcons, and Chicago Bears.

Which cartoon character was voiced by an Arab-American? Was it Shaggy, the slinky, scruffy, hippie friend of Scooby; Fred Flintstone of *The Flintstones*, most famous for bellowing out his wife's name, "Wilmaaaa!"; or the ever genius Homer from *The Simpsons*, with his "Do'h's" and philosophies? While a lot of people often guess Homer, the answer is actually Shaggy. The person who voiced Shaggy is none other than esteemed radio personality and Top 40 host Casey Kasem, originally from Lebanon.

FYI—Lebanon
*You may have noticed that most of the Arab-Americans mentioned were originally from Lebanon. Most Arab immigrants to the United States do come from Lebanon, followed by Egypt, Syria, and Palestine. Some claim themselves as Syrian-Lebanese because the region was historically known as "Greater Syria" until the French and British carved up the remains of the Ottoman Empire after World War I.*

As you can see, there are many Arab-Americans who have made a positive impact on our society, be it in entertainment, sports, politics, medicine, or business.

Congratulations! You have completed the quiz. Let's hope it was helpful. Whatever number you put down for question 1, I hope we managed to move that dial up just a bit. If you thought yourself a 1, I hope you're at least a 3; if you thought yourself a 5, then I hope you're a 7 by now.

# Chapter Seven

# Norms & Mores

## Cultural and Demographic Affairs

THIS SEVENTH CHAPTER OF THE BOOK TRIES to give the reader a sense of the substance of Muslim and Arab-American culture, built up from details as diverse as style of dress, hospitality, and sex.

Topics to be discussed:

- General social norms and mores
- Demographics of the Arab-American community
- The myth and mystery of Arab sexuality
- Contemporary Muslim and Arab dress

Points to remember:

- All norms and mores concerning a community are ultimately generalizations. They are not true for every single member of that community.
- Generally, Muslims and Arabs tend to have a more intimate, more formal, and very hospitable culture.
- Although they tend to keep to themselves, they also blend in with the greater society.
- Current Muslim or Arab attire stretches across the spectrum, everything from traditional robes, dresses, and handmade traditional clothes, to every version of "Western" clothing.

Arab and Muslims cultures are obviously very different from traditional American culture, but conversely are interwoven into the great fabric of America. Part of the challenge of American multiculturalism is that the culture is larger and more varied than what we tend to experience on a daily basis. So it is critical to have a multicultural understanding. That way we can avoid the fear and sometimes the hate that unfortunately tends to come with a lack of understanding. Therefore, it is important to identify and understand what is different in Muslim or Arab culture. On that note, this section will cover some Muslim and Arab social norms and mores to provide information about how Muslims, Arabs or Arab-Americans may behave, in particular during social interaction. Some of these apply to Arab, but not Muslim culture and vice versa.

**General Arab and Muslim Cultural Norms and Mores**

In general, both Muslim and Arab cultures revolve around family, respect, and hospitality. Being gracious and courteous not only with family and friends, but also with strangers, is one of the strongest aspects of Arab culture. Should you have a meeting with an Arab or Muslim, you need to know the following cultural idiosyncrasies so that you are seen as courteous.

When an Arab or Muslim enters the room in formal settings, stand up, look him/her straight in the eye and greet them. Shake his/her hand and, unless told otherwise, refer to him/her by his/her title and last name (Mr., Ms., Dr., and so forth). Formality is standard with first encounters.

Some conservative Muslims do not shake the hands of someone of the opposite sex. (For example, Iraq's Prime Minister Nouri al-Maliki refused to shake hands with the American Secretary of State Condoleeza Rice.) If you are a man, and a woman refuses your hand, place your right hand on your heart. Persons may avoid shaking hands by touching the right hand to the heart, and it is considered polite for you to do the same. This gesture symbolizes a greeting of an open heart to you. However, do not assume because the person appears to be conservative (e.g., a woman wearing a head scarf or a man wearing a skull cap or *kufi*) that the person does not shake hands. It could appear more insulting if you do not offer your hand to a person who does shake hands than if you offer your hand to a person who does not.

Make small talk for the first minute or so. Be sure to ask how the person is doing. Feel free to talk about the weather, the surrounding neighborhood, or other neutral subjects. Do not bring up politics, religion, or conditions that may relate to the government in the person's native country. However, weather-related conditions that have been in the headlines are fine to ask about (e.g, storms, an earthquake). Arabs, for the most part, do not speak about politics with strangers, though political discussions with close friends and family are a norm. This hints at the dichotomy of the private versus public in Arab culture.

If you do not know the Muslim or Arab individual well, be careful in complimenting family, spouse, children, and so forth. This could be construed as inappropriate and is safer to avoid. Should a conversation come up discussing the successes of a family member, such as a son's new job or a daughter's recent soccer win, give generalized statements of support such as "That's wonderful news." This is preferable to, "Wow, she/he is doing so well!"

Be energetic and animated! In general, Muslims and Arabs may regard Americans as stiff and cold. Such attributes are generally read as signs of being dismissive. Keep in mind that just as we have certain stereotypes about their culture, they too have some about ours.

> Point to Ponder
> Their stereotypes about us
>
> So Aladdin and Lawrence of Arabia *have influenced our perception of Arabs. What do you believe has shaped their perceptions of us? Again, it's the great and powerful mass media. If I were to choose dominant pop culture images of the United States in Arab and Muslim pop culture, I would narrow it down to three images:*
>
> 1. *Cowboys—The broad concept of the Old West, six shooters, and John Wayne or Clint Eastwood on horseback.*
>
> 2. *90210—Those five frightening numbers may have affected and misinformed an entire generation, and lead them to believe that we all live like those in that zip code, that we all sleep together, live in lavish mansions, and drive convertibles.*
>
> 3. *Baywatch—Two names: David Hasselhoff and Pamela Anderson.*
>
> *When I was in the Arab world, I grew up watching Dukes of Hazard and only the opening montage of Dallas, as I was apparently too young for the drama. Fortunately, I visited the US from an early age and wasn't expecting the General Lee around every corner.*

When seated, be sure not to cross your legs in a manner that exposes the sole of your shoe. This may be interpreted to mean that you are pointing at a person with your feet, a grave insult in certain Arab and Muslim populations.

When speaking with a person, be sure to make frequent eye contact with him/her. However, eye contact with someone perceived to be in a position of authority over them, be they law enforcement or even a supervisor may not be as frequent. As a show of respect for someone in a position of authority, the person may look them in the eye and look away. So, if they perceive you as an authority, they may look away out of respect. I've always disagreed with the concept of a "clash of civilizations" – I believe, at worst, it's a misunderstanding of civilizations and it's up to those lucky enough to solve the trust formula to share and experience it with others. Be an active listener—smile and nod while the person speaks. Do not fidget at your desk or computer. Do not turn your back to the person. These are all signs of being dismissive and rude.

Questions about religious behavior are considered offensive. Stay away from questions about personal religious practice and participation in mosques. Moreover, as previously mentioned, a follower of the religion of Islam is a Muslim. (This is pronounced Muss-lim with an SSS sound, not Muz-lim or Moz-lem. In some dialects, these last translate as "oppressive" and would not start the meeting off well). Also, avoid other incorrect terms such as "Islamite" or "Mohammedan." If the purpose of your visit is to ask questions relating to a mosque or religious habits, be very respectful and as proper as possible in your demeanor.

Should you be meeting with more than one person, avoid referring to each person by "he" or "she," and instead by "Mr.", "Ms." or "Mrs." (For example, not "He said..." but "Mr. Ibrahim said"). This reiterates the formality within the culture.

When referring to a person in their presence, do not use hand gestures. To call someone over to you, do not motion with your index finger. Pointing is considered as rude in the Arab World as it is here. If you need to gesture, use your entire open hand or arm.

The Arab World gauges personal space differently than do Americans. As a result, Arabs will sometimes get very close to an individual during conversation. Americans sometimes see this person as being aggressive or hostile. However, Arabs communicate as closely as possible. Personal space, our so-called comfort zone in US culture, is roughly ten to twelve inches from nose to nose. In Arab culture it tends to be much closer, roughly six to eight inches, nose to nose. If you feel crowded, or can tell what the other person had for lunch, feel free to step back or ask the person to take a step back. They should not be offended, as chances are they do not even realize what they are doing. I stopped doing this once I realized that most of my students were armed, but I used to lean forward into the front row of my law enforcement classes to make this point on personal space and literally make the officer feel uncomfortable. Ok, I got one kiss out of it, but for the most part, people leaned back.

Generally, Arab culture is far more intimate in all facets of society. For example, people often hug and kiss friends and family each time they see one another. (In some parts of the Arab World these signs of affection may be displayed to same sex only). By contrast, some non-Arab Muslim cultures can be very shy when it comes to personal space. Thus, while many Arabs (Muslim or not) may be very intimate, many non-Arab Muslims, such as Pakistanis, may do very little touching, hugging, and kissing in public. Please remember that these are cultural generalizations and have exceptions.

When persons are leaving, stand up just as you did when they entered the room. Look them in the eye and shake their hands (if they accepted your hand upon first meeting you). Thank them for coming. Once again, formality is imperative.

When visiting an Arab's home, be sure to immediately introduce yourself and explain your reasons for stopping by. Some conservative women (Muslim or not) may not allow a man to enter the house if a male relative is not home, and vice versa. If this is the case, leave your card or contact information and ask when would be a better time to return. In future occasions it may be better to go as a pair, with a man and a woman.

Many Muslim households remove shoes at the door, as rooms with carpeting or rugs are used for prayer. Japanese culture does the same, although for different reasons. If you do not feel comfortable removing your shoes, ask if there is somewhere you could sit and talk without having to remove your shoes.

As hospitality is so highly regarded in Arab culture, most Arabs will try and make you feel at home by offering food and drinks. These are usually sweets (perhaps some baklava or chocolate) and tea or coffee. Even if you do not want to eat or drink anything, accept something small in order to not be seen as insulting your hosts. You are not required to eat or drink the item once it is accepted.

An important aspect of giving compliments must be emphasized. Make no exaggerated compliments. Due to the overt hospitality in Arab culture, bear in mind that if you strongly compliment or admire an Arab's possession, that person may feel obliged to give you that possession as a gift, even if it is dear to him or her. This is by no means a ploy to get rich: "Nice Ferrari!" *hands keys over*. Material compliments should be sincere, but never over the top.

When interacting with Muslims, show proper respect for the *Quran*. If you do not need to handle the *Quran*, do not do so. If you do handle the *Quran*, do not write on it, place anything on top of it, or place it on the floor. Treat it as you would any other holy book, with respect. It is common for Muslims to have Qurans in numerous places in the home, in their cars, or even in luggage or purses.

It is also common for Muslims and Arabs (irrespective of their faith) to use religious language in everyday conversation. They do it in greetings, business dealings, and regular social interactions. Even Muslims who are not speaking Arabic may use certain Arabic phrases or statements throughout their conversation. A reference to God is always near the conversation. For example, a regular "Hey, how's it going?" conversation could go something as follows:

> Person A: *Greetings and salutations and peace be upon you and the mercy of God.*
> Person B: *And peace be to you too and the mercy of God.*
> Person A: *How have you been?*
> Person B: *Thanks be to God, I am doing well. And you?*
> Person A: *Thanks be to God, I am well too.*

There are a select few religious buzzwords in Arabic that may be stated in English as part of the conversation. *Inshallah*—"God willing"—is used often in everyday conversation. "*Would you like to grab lunch?*" "*Yes, God willing,*" is not atypical. *Bismillah al Rahman al Raheem*—"In the name of God most merciful, most gracious," (sometimes limited to only *Bismillah*, "In the name of God") is often used as a short prayer before eating or starting an act. *Hamdillah* or *Hamdulillah*—"Thank God"— are also used regularly in everyday conversation. Thanking God after a

meal or most events is accepted as normal. *Mashallah*—"By the will of God"—is usually used as a reaction to something positive taking place. For example, if Person A shares with Person B the fact that her child earned straight A's in school, Person B can reply *Mashallah*.

Arabs tend to be a very proud and courteous people. Muslim and Arab cultures are filled with pride, honor, and self-respect. This is partly due to the great history from which Muslims and Arabs come. Do your best to be respectful. In circumstances that may involve humiliation, both Muslims and Arabs will prefer to save face and be discreet about it. Keep in mind that the family is a very important part of Arab culture. In some cases a Muslim, Arab or Arab-American may prefer to hold an interview in the presence of the family.

Generally speaking, Muslim and Arab families tend to be patriarchal. The father, or sometimes the grandfather, usually holds a position of power and authority over the family. Very high levels of respect exist for the family patriarch. In addition, the elderly are held in the highest esteem. Again, these are generalizations, my family was always very matriarchal, both my grandmothers were leaders and my mom… well, you've seen all the influence she's had on her surroundings just from this book. To quote "My Big Fat Greek Wedding"—which may as well have been reflecting Muslim or Arab cultures, "the man is the head of the house, but the woman is the neck, and she can turn the head any way she wants."

These points are very important as they will help the individual break the ice. Once that ice is broken, trust can be secured. Once both individuals learn to trust one another, there is no limit as to what can be gained.

It should also be noted that while countries like Saudi Arabia until 2018 required women to cover up in public, irrespective of their beliefs or faith, other Muslim countries, such as Turkey, forbid veiled women or men with "religious beards" from working in any government or public buildings. However, that typically is not an image we see of Muslim countries.

FYI – La la la la laa!
*Many of you may have seen images of Arab women, celebrating at weddings, going "La la la la laa!" with their hands over their mouths. This is called ululating, and it is cultural. It is a tradition that traces back to old times when the women would celebrate by sounding off for the bride, then serenading her with a spontaneous poem. The television show, Family Guy, seemingly made this act infamous, when Stewie asks an apparent Arab/Muslim terrorist: "I say, Akmed, what's that thing you people do when you're about to assassinate an infidel?" Comedy gold and while I love the show because it makes fun of everything and everyone, it's of course wholly inaccurate. True story. I was speaking to a group of analysts in the South one year and a gentleman who seemed quiet and perhaps apprehensive all day finally spoke his first sentence while I was discussing ululating and as I did the sound, he interjected: "You did that awfully well," which made me laugh as I restated it's NOT a terrorist death call.*

FYI—Rhythm
*Here's an Arab joke: Put three Arabs in a room, and it becomes a party. Generally, Arabs tend to share a sense of rhythm and soul. Often when Arabs are applauding, random clapping becomes one unified sound. It highlights the common rhythm often found in Arab culture, and shared with many other cultures.*

## Traditional and Current Arab Dress

What is traditional Arab dress? Well, many Arabs today wear some form

of modern Western dress, from plain jeans and tee-shirts to three-piece suits to the latest fashions from Paris or Milan. Others wear various forms of traditional attire, often due to the climate and custom. Islamic attire generally follows the local culture, be it Arab or Indian or Nigerian, for that matter. Islam simply states modesty for both men and women. The rest is cultural interpretation of the faith.

Men in Saudi Arabia and the Gulf States tend to wear traditional headwear that includes a *ghutra*, a large, diagonally folded cotton square, plain white, or checkered with black or red. This is held in place by an *igaal*, which looks like a fancy rope border around the top of the head and acts as a weight over the cloth.[89] Men and women in the Levant region, (the area including Syria, Lebanon, Jordan, Palestine, and parts of Iraq) do not usually wear the *ghutra*. Instead, they wear a *kufi*, *kufiyeh*, or *hut-ta*—usually a checkered cloth, black and white or red and white, worn not as a headpiece, but more often as a shawl or scarf. This is not a political statement, although some have tried to make it so, and one wearing it is simply expressing their culture or being fashionable. I used to ski with mine just for fun. The conversation piece it became was hilarious and oh people are so friendly, they would immediately ask me to go ahead of them in line! I always laughed at the "so, where ya from?" question. When I would say West Virginia, it rarely seemed to satisfy, and I'd get the "where are you really from?" follow-up.

Men in North Africa do not traditionally wear any form of headscarf or turban, although you may find local and traditional influences and exceptions. Occasionally you may see older North African men wearing a fez or *sheysheh*, usually as part of wedding attire. The fez is a remnant of the Ottoman Empire, which ruled that whole region into southern Europe for close to eight hundred years. In other parts of the Arab World, the fez is known as the *tarboosh*.

Some Arab men wear the *thawb* or *gallabeya*, a simple, ankle-length shirt of wool or cotton. While part of culture and tradition, this garment is also practical for those who live in the heat and/or desert where the *thawb* flows freely in the wind and helps cool the person. Other men wear a flowing, floor-length outer cloak, known as a *bisht* or *abaya*. These are made of wool or camel hair in black, beige, brown, or cream tones. Perhaps because of Americans' familiarity with Scottish kilts, I am sometimes asked whether the men wear anything underneath these long garments. The answer is yes—the material is usually thick enough that it cannot be seen through, but men tend to wear undershirts of some form and underwear at the very least. Occasionally loose, short pants are worn underneath. Traditionally, these clothing styles were very practical and comfortable in an often-harsh climate. In the strong winds of the desert, air could keep one cool. The head coverings (worn in public by both men and women) protect wearers from the strong sunlight.

Women's attire also ranges across the spectrum. Women across the Arab World wear modern attire, including business suits, skirts, shorts, and formal gowns. Others will be dressed more traditionally in the *abaya* or even more conservative garb such as the *burqa*.

Women in Islam are expected to be modest (as are men) and are required to cover up during prayer. Depending on the region and their personal preference, some women choose to wear a veil or *hijab*. In some countries, women in public choose a more conservative veil that is tight around the head and worn along with an overcoat. Still, others choose different color veils, and mix and match with modern attire. Beyond veils, women in the Arab World may also wear traditional long flowing dresses called *gallabeya*. Similar to the *abaya*, this is related to the men's version but not the same. In some localities women will wear a *burqa* or *niqab*, which also covers the face. Note that this is a cultural and political interpretation of the faith.

Remember, all Americans do not wear cowboy hats, large belt buckles, or ball caps. But for those who do, it is merely an expression of themselves and their culture through their attire.

## Images of Muslim and Arab Sexuality

A subject that must be explored at least briefly is the image of Arab sexuality. *The Thousand and One Nights* and the adventures of *Scheherazade* are famous and, to some, sexually enticing. They have been translated into numerous languages over the centuries. Although these works in particular date back to the tenth century, many parts were a mixture of Arab, Persian, and Indian folk tales combined by Arab authors to become known ultimately as *The Arabian Nights*.

The durability of these ancient folk tales suggests that the Arab possesses a certain allure, in particular the Arab woman. The concept of a harem is also appealing and intriguing, perhaps particularly to societies where polygamy is outlawed. Additionally, because little is known about the Muslims and Arabs, the sexual side is treated with anticipation and uncertainty. A record of Internet searches about Arabs suggests that images of Arab sexuality hold an unusually high attraction and curiosity. Interestingly enough, the most searched phrase associated with the term "Arab" on the Internet is *Arab sex*.[90] Of the most searched terms associated with the term "Arab," over 40% are in one way or another related to sex, including *Arab nude, Arab girl, Arab gay, Arab porn, Arab woman*, and *sexy Arab*.[91] This is very interesting, as there seems to be an attraction and curiosity toward the unknown world of the Arabs.

After discovering that the top Internet search term associated with Arab was "Arab sex," I decided to search a variety of other terms to see if sex was always the most searched term. After all, the online porn industry is one that exceeds ninety-seven billion dollars annually and is constantly growing. I searched Italian, Finnish, German, Mexican, Korean, French, and American.[92] All had sex somewhere in the top twenty, but none had it as the top term:

Italian: *learn Italian*

Finnish: *Finnish sauna*

German: *learn German*

Mexican: *Mexican recipe*

Korean: *travel Korean*

French: *learn French*

American: *American Idol*

After doing a number of searches, most came up with "learn _____," as in "learn Russian," or "learn Japanese." The only other term to have "sex" as the highest searched phrase was "Indian." Interestingly enough, the two cultures, although different, do share some history and tradition. More importantly, similar to Arab culture, Indian culture is treated with that same sort of alluring mystery. Perhaps unsurprisingly, one of the most searched and most famous adult movie stars is Lebanese-born Arab-American Mia Khalifa, though she clarifies she is not Muslim, but was raised Catholic.

It is ironic that although there is a stereotype of Muslims being sexually repressed, Muslims and Arabs are still represented as exotic sexual beings. Depending on where you are in the Muslim or Arab World, the degree to which public displays of affection are accepted varies greatly. Dating, though it is most definitely taking place among the younger generations, is generally not discussed openly. Physical affection and sex are expected to be limited to married couples. Depending on the country, violations can be punished by law. Once a couple is married, they are encouraged to explore their sexuality and please one another in private.

In most instances, when conducting a security search of an Arab or Muslim, it is best to ask if the person would prefer someone from the same gender to do the search. A conservative Muslim, man or woman, would expect this. If a woman wearing a veil must be searched, this should be done by another woman, and in private. If her veil needs to be removed, it should also be in private where strange men cannot see her.

Some Arab countries are beginning to accept expressions of sexuality in public. Lebanon seems to lead that charge and has become very "Westernized" in that respect. A colleague of mine used to joke that the reason

Italians and Spaniards are known as great lovers is because the Arabs were in those lands for more than eight hundred years. In other words, it's in their blood. The point is that the passionate and exotic image of Italians and Spaniards holds true for Arabs as well.

**By the Numbers—Statistical Breakdown of Muslims and Arab-Americans**

The following is critical statistical information about the Arab-American community.

- There are approximately 3.7 million Arab-Americans.[93, 94]
- Approximately 82% of Arabs in the United States are American citizens.[95]
- 59% of Arab-Americans were born in the United States.[96]
- 21% of those not born in the United States are naturalized citizens[97]
- 19% are not yet citizens[98]
- 25% Lebanese [99,100]
- 12% Egyptian[101]
- 8% Syrian[102]
- 6% Palestinian[103]
- 4% Jordanian[104]
- 5% Assyrian/Chaldean (direct descendants of the ancient Assyrians and Babylonians)
- 5% Moroccan[105]
- 6% Iraqi[106]
- 8% from Algeria, Bahrain, Comoros Islands, Djibouti, Kuwait, Libya, Mauritania, Oman, Qatar, Saudi Arabia, Sudan, Tunisia, the United Arab Emirates, or Yemen[107]
- 16% "Arab"[108] – Country of origin not specified
- Most live in California, Michigan, New York, Texas, and Florida
- 48% live in twenty metropolitan areas[109]
- Those Arabs living in Fairfax County in Virginia, along with Macomb and Wayne counties in Michigan, make up 2% to 3%

of the entire Arab-American population.[110]

- The metropolitan areas with the largest Arab-American populations are Los Angeles, Detroit, New York City, and Washington, DC, respectively.[111]

- 42% Catholic[112]
- 23% Eastern Orthodox[113]
- 12% Protestant[114]
- 23% Muslim[115]

- 84% have at least a high school diploma (the national average is 80%)[116]
- 41% hold a bachelor's degree or higher (the national average is 24.4%)[117]
- 15% hold graduate degrees[118]

- 73% of Arab-Americans aged sixteen and older hold some form of employment (higher than the national average of 71%).[119]
- 42% of working adults are employed in professional or managerial fields (higher than the national average of 34%).[120]
- 77% work in the private sector[121]
- 12.4% are government employees[122]
- 5.9% are unemployed[123]

- Muslims in America are estimated at just under 4 million. Per the Pew Research Center, the numbers are changing and about 31% are college graduates, including 11% with postgraduate degrees. Approximately 58% of Muslims in America are first generation; 18% are second generation; and 24% are third generation or more (US born with US born parents). Counties of origin vary, but about 20% are of South Asian descent (Pakistan, India, Afghanistan, Bangladesh); 14% are Middle East North Africa, 6% Iranian and 5% Sub-Saharan African. Three in ten Muslim immigrants arrived in the U.S. since 2010. Conversion rates are high and the numbers continue to change. Per Pew, 41% of Muslim Americans are "White"—but this counts the absurd census counting of MENA (Middle East North African)

Americans as White. I have never felt "White" in my life. This dated label goes back to a 1915 appellate case that deemed a Syrian man immigrating as White. The community embraced it, as being labeled Asian or African would have hindered their immigration efforts. A century later, it is time to count us for who we are, a diverse, unique, separate community with our own history and demographics.

# Chapter Eight

# Muslims and Arabs in US History

## Historical, Geographical, and Linguistic Affairs.

THIS EIGHTH CHAPTER OF THE BOOK TRACES THE history of Muslims and Arabs in North and South America.

Topics to be discussed:

- Early Arab voyages to the New World
- History of Muslims and Arab-Americans, including slavery
- World Geography
- Arabic influence on the English, French and Spanish languages

Points to remember:

- Evidence suggests Arabs arrived at our shores as early as the 1500s.
- There have been two primary waves of immigration: the first in the late nineteenth century and the second in the mid-twentieth century through the present.
- There are approximately one thousand English and French words and several thousand Spanish words derived from Arabic. You probably know more Arabic than you realize.

### Early Arab & Muslim Americans

Arabs and Muslims have been coming to what is today the United States since the late 1500s. They have fought and died in every US war dating back to the Revolutionary War. Some historical experts believe that the first Arab settler in North America was a shipwrecked passenger who landed on the island of Okracoke just off the coast of North Carolina in the mid-1600s.[124] According to the authors of *The Arab Americans*,

"Family tradition holds that the Wahab family of Okracoke Island, thirty miles off the coast of North Carolina, descends from the first Wahab sent as an emissary of the 'King of Arabia' in the mid-seventeenth century to establish the Muslim religion in the New World."[125] Shipwrecked with a load of Arabian horses on the outer banks of North Carolina, Wahab established "Wahab Village," which today is the site of an inn that is still run by the Wahab family.

Other records show that the first Arab in North America was an Andalusian. (Remember Andalusia was Arab Spain, which existed for roughly eight hundred years). He was known only as Esteban, his Christian name. Like many other Muslims and Jews, Esteban converted to Christianity to avoid being expelled by the Spanish government after 1492. Esteban reached what is now Florida in 1528.[126] He learned the dialects and customs of many of the Native American tribes along the Gulf of Mexico. In 1539 he led the Conquistadors into the present states of New Mexico and Arizona in search of the "Seven Cities of Cibola." The Native American Pueblo peoples understandably did not welcome the intrusion. Esteban himself was killed by the Zunis, whose descendants today remember him in the form of a Kachina in their religious tradition.[127]

Others believe that Christopher Columbus's navigator was an Arab. (Apparently, he was not very good though, as they were trying to get to India!) In fact, the Pinzon brothers, the owners and captains of the Nina and the Pinta, were Andalusians. The Pinzon family was related to Abuzayan Muhammad III (1362—66), the Moroccan sultan of the Marinid dynasty (1196—1465). Arabs made many advances in navigation and navigational tools. They were skilled and successful sea travelers and merchants.

Another of the early arrivals was a Chaldean priest, Father Elms from Mosul, Iraq. He arrived in the Americas in 1668 and traveled here for fifteen years, journeying through the booming Spanish-American communities and ending in Mexico.[128]

Many victims of the slave trade triangle brought to the New World against their will were Arabs and/or Muslims from Africa. (Remember that most Arabs are also African; most Arabs live in the continent of Africa). Arab slaves? Absolutely. Muslim slaves? Absolutely. Consequently, a great number of Arabs were slaves. An estimated 20% to 30% of the slaves brought to the United States were Muslim. Slaves with names such as Omar Ibn-Said, Job Ben-Solomon, Paul Labman Kibby, Prince Omar, and Ben Ali were brought here as slaves.[129] While the vast majority of slaves were forced to practice Christianity, many kept Islamic traditions that you can still find today in several African-American churches along the eastern seaboard and in the Deep South. However, many of the worshipers don't recognize the origin of those traditions. Some of them include avoiding pork products, facing east to pray (and in some cases building the church so that the structure faces east), using prayer rugs, and naming children traditional Muslim names such as Mohammed, Jamal, Zainab, and Aisha. Often, slaves used Arabic as a secret language to plot revolts and escapes. Whether they were Arab or Muslim, they would have known enough Arabic to worship in Arabic. Among the pop culture famous stories based on real events was that of Amistad, where slaves in 1893 led a mutiny against the ship with the title name. Those slaves were members of the Mandinga (sometimes called Mandingo or Mandinka) tribe, many of the slaves, estimates go as high as 25% were Mandinga and about 95% of the tribe were Muslim.

FYI—Andalusia—Muslim Spain

*In 711, the Umayyad (or Ummawiy) empire based in Damascus, Syria had stretched to the borders of India and China eastward and spanned North Africa westward. An oppressed Christian chief, Julian, went to Musa Ibn Nusair, the governor of North Africa, pleading for help against the tyrannical Visigoth ruler of Spain, Roderick. Musa responded by sending the young general Tariq Bin Ziyad with an army of 7,000 troops to face the Visigoths. The name Gibraltar is derived from Jabal Tariq, which is Arabic for "Mount Tariq," named after the place where the Muslim army landed.*

*The Muslim invasion, and subsequent administration of Iberia, freed the Spanish population of Jews from Visigothic oppression. It was said that immediately after the invasion, the Jewish population of Toledo opened the gates of the city, welcoming the Arab Muslims. Though prevailing warriors, the Muslims were full of honor and chivalry. They gave the Goth Spaniards an opportunity to surrender each of their provinces, to which most agreed. This was a tactic seen again and again in battles where Muslims gained the upper hand. They would often offer peace and the right to live among them, if the opposing army laid down its arms and accepted peace (never forcefully converting Christians or Jews, as they are "People of the Book.") Salah El-Din (Saladin), the great Muslim leader who regained Jerusalem from the Crusaders, was famous for such acts of kindness and chivalry. And so Andalusia flourished for about 800 years, until January 2, 1492 (more than one thing happened that year!), when Ferdinand and Isabella expelled all the Jews and Muslims and the Arab influence withered. Andalusia was Arab, it was Muslim, and it hosted the peaceful and fruitful coexistence of Jews, Christians, and Muslims where a great civilization thrived in science, literature, and architecture that helped usher in the rebirth (Renaissance) from the Dark Ages in Europe. I sometimes ask my audience if they know what is "Andalusia". People either know it or they don't. I was once speaking in the Midwest to a group of FBI agents and upon asking that question a very enthusiastic hand shoots up with the gentlemen exclaiming: "That's my hometown!" Lesson learned for me, there is apparently a beautiful little town in Alabama with less than 10,000 people that shares the same name.*

In 1790, the South Carolina House of Representatives allowed Moors, subjects of the Emperor of Morocco, to be tried in court according to the laws of its citizens, and not under slave codes. Like others forced into slavery, these Arabic-speaking people, over generations, lost ties with their former culture.[130]

Larger numbers of Arabs began settling in the United States toward the end of the nineteenth century, attracted like most other immigrants by economic and educational opportunities. Today, the majority of Arab-Americans are descendants of the first wave of primarily Christian Syrian and Lebanese immigrants. This wave began in the mid-to-late nineteenth century and lasted through the early twentieth century. As a direct result of this wave of immigration, 77% of Arab-Americans today identify themselves as Christian, despite the majority of Arabs worldwide being Muslim.

Immigration to the United States was restricted following World War I. The second wave of Arab immigrants did not begin until after World

War II. This second wave also primarily consisted of Syrians and Lebanese, though Palestinians, Jordanians, Yemenis, Iraqis, and Egyptians also made their way to the States. These first two waves of immigrants came largely from rural areas and had limited amounts of formal education. In the 1970s, political tensions in the Middle East were high and the United States began loosening immigration laws. Consequently, the immigration trends from the Arab World began to diversify: more Arab Muslims began immigrating, as well as Arabs from urban areas and with higher educational backgrounds.[131]

Today, Arab-Americans are present in each state of the union, in every field of employment, from factories to hospitals to Hollywood. By now you have learned that Arab-Americans have fought and died in every war and military conflict, from the Revolutionary War to the conflict in Iraq. An Arab-American is responsible for the creation of the ice cream cone, the first artificial heart, and the American Top 40 Countdown.[132]

### Arab and Muslim Influence on the United States

Although often not openly recognized, the Arab World and the Muslim faith have influenced much in our American culture. So much of what is today labeled as "American" traces its roots to the Arab Muslim world. Let me explain:

The Spanish who settled in the southern part of the North American continent transported designs, materials, and food inspired by Arab Muslims, who ruled and influenced Spain for over eight hundred years.[133] Typical "southwestern" architecture, such as enclosed patios, fountains, and arches were brought here by way of Arab Muslim Spain: Andalusia.

Some Native American historians believe that certain Native American jewelry (specifically types of Navajo jewelry) was originally influenced by Spanish-Arab-Muslim Mudejars.[134] The squash blossom necklace looks like an inverted crescent and was apparently influenced by a design adopted from Muslim ornaments of the crescent. The crescent moon is the symbol of Islam as the cross is the symbol for Christianity and the six-sided star for Judaism.[135]

FYI—Mudejars
*Mudejars were Arab Muslims who stayed after the fall of Andalusia in 1492, when most Muslims and Jews left or were*

*forced out. Those who remained were forced to convert to Christianity. However, many Muslims (Mudejars, also called Moriscos, "little Moors") and Jews (Marranos) observed their faiths in secret, pretending to be Christian in public. Most also took Christian names.*

Who would have thought that the all-American image of the cowboy was actually influenced by Arabs and Muslims? The Mudejars were skilled horsemen and brought over the saddle, spurs, and even the boots to the United States.[136] Donald Chaves, a New Mexican author and cowboy historian, has stated that the pointed-toed, high-heeled, and high-topped boots that Americans identify as cowboy boots were designed by Muslims in Andalusia. Moreover, the intricate stitching is reminiscent of the decorative Arab designs.[137]

## Geography and the World

In November of 2002, the National Geographic Society published what ultimately was an embarrassing report about the United States' younger generation. A survey conducted in nine countries asked fifty-six questions about geography and current events. Those surveyed were ages eighteen to twenty-four, the prime age for the military, and the results were troubling, to say the least. Bear in mind that, at the time the survey was administered, the US military had been in Afghanistan for approximately a year. In addition, although we had not yet begun fighting Operation Iraqi Freedom, thousands of soldiers had been stationed in the vicinity of Iraq since Operation Desert Storm from the early 1990s. The United States passed with a "D" average, barely ahead of Mexico, which came in last place.[138]

Findings from the survey included the following:

- 87% of Americans surveyed could not find Iraq on a map. (The same was true for Iran.)

- 83% could not find Afghanistan on a map. (We had already been there for a year.)

- 76% could not find Saudi Arabia on a map.

- 70% could not find New Jersey on a map. (I know we pick on it, but come on.)

- 49% could not find the state of New York on a map. (The nation's fourth most populous state.)

- 11% could not find the United States on a map. (Even though our nation takes up half a continent.)

In April 2006, the National Geographic Society conducted a second survey of geography and Americans.[139] Sadly, the numbers are still disappointing. In fact in certain cases, they were worse:

- 88% could not find Afghanistan. (At this point, the United States had been there more than four years.)

- 63% could not find Iraq or Saudi Arabia.

- 75% could not find Iran.

- 50% could not find New York State.

As of September 2016, yet another survey with similar concerning results. "The global literacy survey asked 1,203 young adults 75 questions about geography. Among 18—26-year-olds who attend or have attended a two-or four-year college in the United States, the average score on the survey was just 55%—a failing grade in most US classrooms".[140]

Why am I sharing this? We, as Americans, need to be aware of ourselves and our surroundings. The results of these surveys are not only disappointing, but also frightening. One of the basic steps to reach a better understanding of those who are different from us is to learn about their existence and their homeland as they would about ours. Because of this study, I always bring a world map with me to class so that I can point out the countries I talk about. For your added insight, feel free to review a world map at www.cia.gov/the-world-factbook/maps/.

## Arabic in Your English, Spanish & French

There are approximately one thousand words in the English language derived from Arabic. The same is true for French. Moreover, because the Iberian Peninsula (present-day Spain and Portugal) was Arab for over eight hundred years (Andalusia), there are around 4,000 Spanish words that are ultimately derived from Arabic. Therefore, chances are that you speak more Arabic than you realize. Feel free to update your resumes under "Languages" and list "Arabic: Fluent" It may greatly improve your career upward mobility! It is good to learn about these words in order to further understand our culture.

Listed below are a few words with their Arabic origins and meanings. For some of these words, Arabic is not the original root, but it was through the spread of the Arabic language that the words made it to English. Also remember, "al" is merely the Arabic word for "the."[141]

| | | |
|---|---|---|
| Admiral: | *amir al* | Ruler of; originally "amir al-bahr," ruler of the sea. |
| Alchemy: | *alkimia* | Greek "chemia," a pouring together. |
| Alcohol: | *al-kuhoul* | Powder of antimony, used to color the eyebrows. |
| Alcove: | *al-gobbah* | Vault, arch, dome. |
| Alfalfa: | *al-fac, facah* | The best fodder. |
| Algebra: | *al-jabr* | The reunion of broken parts, from "jabara," reunite. |
| Almanac: | *almanakh* | Almanac or calendar. |
| Amber: | *'anbar* | Grey amber. |
| Arsenal: | *dar as-sina' ah* | Workshop, literally, house of skill or trade. |
| Azure: | *lazward* | Sky blue, from Persian word *lazhward.* |
| Candy: | *qandi* | Made of sugar. |
| Calibre: | *kaleb* | Mold or cast. |
| Cipher: | *sifr* | Cipher, nothing. |
| Coffee: | *qahwa* | Coffee. |
| Cotton: | *qutun* | Cotton. |
| Crimson: | *qermez* | Crimson, from Sanskrit *krmija.* |
| Elixir: | *el iksir* | The philosopher's stone. |

| Gazelle: | *gazal* | Gazelle. |
|---|---|---|
| Jar: | *jarrah* | Water vessel. |
| Julep: | *julab* | Persian *gulab*, rose water. |
| Lemon: | *laymoun* | Lemon. |
| Magazine: | *makhzan* | Storehouse. |
| Mattress: | *matrah* | Mattress, foundation, place where anything is thrown. |
| Muslin: | *Mawsil* | Mosul, a city in Iraq where the first muslin was made. |
| Ream: | *rizmat* | Bale, a packet, especially a ream of paper; from "razama." |
| Saffron: | *za'faran* | Saffron. |
| Sahara: | *sahra* | Desert. |
| Sash: | *shash* | Turban. |
| Satin: | *Zaitun* | Medieval name of Chinese city, Tsinkiang |
| Sherbet: | *sherbet* | *sharaba*, to drink. |
| Sheriff: | *sharrif* | Honorable one—because it was the honor-able one who enforced the law. |
| Sofa: | *soffah* | Cushion or saddle. |
| Sugar: | *sakkar* | Persian *shakar* and Sanskrit *carkara*, candied sugar. |
| Syrup: | *sharab* | *Shariba*, drink. |
| Tariff: | *tar'if* | Explanation, information, a list of things, especially of fees to be paid; from *arafa*, to inform. |
| Zenith: | *semt-ar-ras* | Zenith, literally *way of the head*. |
| Zero: | *sifr* | Cipher. |

FYI—Yalla

*Literally Ya Allah, which means "oh God." It has become a collo-quial term meaning, "Let's go." In certain situations, there have been examples of non-Arabic speakers adopting and using the word.*

With regard to the Spanish language, Gerald Erichsen, an active online Spanish editor and translator, has written, "It is not 'real' Arabic you are speaking, but rather words that come from Arabic. After Latin and English, Arabic is probably the biggest contributor of words to the Spanish language, and a large portion of English-Spanish cognates (words that the two languages share) that do not come from Latin come from Arabic."

"The etymology of English words," Erichsen continues, "goes beyond the scope of this article, but the introduction of Arabic words into Spanish began in earnest in the eighth century, although even before then some words of Latin and Greek origin had roots in Arabic. People living in what is now Spain spoke Latin at one time, of course, but over the centuries Spanish and other Romance languages such as French and Italian gradually differentiated themselves. The Latin dialect that eventually became Spanish was highly influenced by the invasion of the Arabic-speaking Moors in 711. For many centuries, Latin/Spanish and Arabic existed side by side, and even today many Spanish place names retain Arabic roots. It was not until late in the 15th century that the Moors were expelled. By then literally thousands of Arabic words had become part of Spanish."[142] As an example of place names, Guadalajara is derived from the Arabic term Wadi Al-Hijara or *Valley of the rocks*.

> FYI—Who were the Moors?
> *"Moor" was another term for Arabs, mostly from North Africa. When the Romans entered Africa in 46 BC, they saw local people and called them Maures, from the Greek adjective mauros, meaning dark or black. It is from these meanings that the term "Moor" is derived. Because the inhabitants of North Africa had darker skins, the Romans and later the Europeans called them Moors, i.e. the Darks.[143] Fun fact, Salvador Dali was apparently convinced he was of Moorish heritage, identified as Arab ethnically, and weaved inspiration from these beliefs into his art.*

It was as late as 1567 that Philip II of Spain issued a royal decree banning all use of Arabic, be it spoken or written, formal or informal settings. Up until then, one could easily find both Spanish and Portuguese languages written in Arabic script. Pretty amazing! This was known as Aljamiado or Aljamia.

*Note: For more on the importation of Muslims from Africa to the US as slaves, see* Muslims in American History *by Jerald F. Dirks.*

# Conclusion

I N THE POST-9/11 WORLD, MUSLIMS, ARABS, and Arab-Americans, and those perceived to be such have been mislabeled and sometimes victimized because of their national origin, ethnicity, faith, and even appearance. We must remember that, like so many of our American brothers and sisters, Arabs and Muslims are part of the fabric that was woven together to create our United States. They helped build what President Reagan called The Shining City on a Hill. A beacon of freedom and liberty and wonder that is a signal and an example to the rest of the world. Arabs and Muslims are embedded in our great history and culture.

If we inherently alter our way of life and ultimately try to choose between security and liberty, then we will have changed the foundation of this nation and the bad actors will have indeed won. A healthy balance between liberty and security has made the United States a global success. We are the spiritual descendent of Andalusia. Today, with our unparalleled technological advances, our world-best academic institutions, our military might, and our overall dominant culture, we are an evolution of what Andalusia was to the known world. If we change the essence of our liberty and all that our nation has stood for over the past several centuries, we will have lost the war, regardless of how many battles we win. The vision of our Founding Fathers will have died and the United States' stance as a beacon of freedom and opportunity across our world will have mutated into a closed off and frightened society. It is critical to note that one of the greatest and most powerful empires in history, the Roman Empire, was not destroyed by an external army. It did not collapse from an invading force. Rather, it deteriorated and disintegrated from within. We as a nation and as a society cannot afford to go down a similar path and ultimately make a similar mistake. No matter how terrible our challenges may appear, we must remain steadfast in the face of adversity and controversy. We must learn from history and maintain our courage. Otherwise, we are bound to make the same mistakes.

I hope this book has been helpful and achieved the goal I set out for it as an introductory guide to the Muslim, Arab, and Arab-American communities. I hope it shed some much-needed light on the subjects at hand and, for lack of better terms, that it humanized and demystified these communities so that you could better understand them.

I hope this book has stimulated your thirst for information and will allow you to go about your responsibilities in your professional and personal life with added appreciation and insight about these communities, that it will make you want to learn more about them from accurate sources. I hope that you are now able to tell who is an Arab and a Muslim, what they are all about, both physically and that which exists beneath the surface; that you are not so quick to judge or label or even blame or hate; and that you now have developed a new appreciation for Muslims, Arabs, and Arab-Americans, and their respective cultures.

You now know that Arabs come in many different appearances and "colors," that they practice many different faiths, and that they are not one large homogenous cohesive unit, but a diverse and multi-hued, heterogeneous, multiracial people, whose origins extend as far east as Oman, as far west as Mauritania and Morocco, as far south as Sudan, and as far north as Algeria, Tunisia, Syria, and Iraq.

You now know that most Muslims are not Arab but rather from South Asia and South East Asia, that Muslims currently live all over the world. You also now know that Muslims believe that Islam is a continuation of the holy faiths of Moses and Jesus, Judaism and Christianity, respectively. You now know what is the real meaning of *jihad*, and who Allah really is to any Arabic speaking person. You also now know some basic cultural norms and mores and methods. Hopefully these can help break the proverbial ice and, in certain cases, melt an entire glacier.

Ultimately, when all is said and done, the goal was to provide a thorough and detailed introduction to these communities. In the post-9/11 world, they have been at the center of a lot of attention, much of it negative and speculative. Perhaps now these communities can be better understood. The formula once again is simple:

Understanding + Communication = Trust

Lack of trust is our greatest challenge. Once we achieve trust between the communities and their government, together we can achieve so much. I see this book as a civil servant of some sort trying to take necessary steps to improve communication and understanding, and therefore ultimately to gain and maintain trust. I hope this book has helped with understanding and will lead to better trust. The next step of communication falls partly on your shoulders.

I choose to end with a brief section of *Quotes & Notes*. It is made up of various quotations from history and other sources that apply to this book. For some of the quotations, I felt the need to elaborate and provide my own input, influence, or explanation. I hope you will appreciate them and learn from them as much as I.

# Quotes & Notes

*People are unreasonable, illogical, and self-centered. Love them anyway. If you are kind, people may accuse you of selfish motives. Be kind anyway. If you are successful, you may win false friends and true enemies. Succeed anyway. The good you do today may be forgotten tomorrow. Do good anyway. Honesty and transparency make you vulnerable. Be honest and transparent anyway. What you spend years building may be destroyed overnight. Build anyway. People who really want help may attack you if you help them. Help them anyway. If you find serenity and happiness, others may be jealous. Be happy anyway. Give the world the best you have and you may get hurt. Give the world your best anyway. You see, in the final analysis, it is between you and God; it was never between you and them anyway.*
—Mother Teresa

*We will not be driven by fear into an age of unreason.*
—Edward R. Murrow

This quote by the famed journalist signifies my belief that more information, more knowledge, and more understanding is needed and necessary to combat the growing fear, confusion, and hate.

*We can easily forgive a child who is afraid of the dark. The real tragedy of life is when men are afraid of the light.*
—Plato

*We must scrupulously guard the civil rights and civil liberties of all citizens, whatever their background. We must remember that any oppression, any injustice, any hatred, is a wedge designed to attack our civilization.*
—President Franklin Delano Roosevelt, 1940

President Roosevelt's sentiment applies to Arab and Muslim-Americans today.

*They that can give up essential liberty to obtain a little temporary security deserve neither liberty nor security.*
—Benjamin Franklin, 1759

In 1759, when Franklin spoke, the United States was not yet a nation. Liberty would become a founding pillar of this country. We should understand that liberty and security are not mutually exclusive.

*Are you a politician asking what your country can do for you or a zealous one asking what you can do for your country? If you are the first, then you are a parasite; if the second, then you are an oasis in the desert.*
—Khalil Gibran, 1925

Gibran was one of the most famous Arab-Americans of the twentieth century. This particular quote was later reworked and attributed to President John F. Kennedy as part of his famous "Ask not what you can do for your country..." speech.

*True servants of the Compassionate (God) are those who walk the earth in humility and when ignorant people address them, they reply with words of peace.*
—*The Holy Quran*, 25:63

*In valor, there is hope.*
—Publius Cornelius Tacitus, 55-120 AD

*Before today, I used to criticize my companion if my religion was not the one which he followed. But my heart changed to accept every image, so pastures for the carefree lovers and convents for the monks. A house of idols and the idol house at Taa'if, the tablets of the Torah and the mushaf of the Quran. I follow the religion of love wherever it takes me, so all religion is my religion and belief.*
—Ibn 'Arabi, *Dhakhaairul-A'laaq*

This is from Ibn 'Arabi, the twelfth century Arab philosopher. His intent is self-explanatory and provides a deeper look inside the mind of this famed Arab and Muslim intellectual. What his thought states is true Islam, the understanding and continuation of Judaism and Christianity.

*Excellence is the result of caring more than others think is wise; risking more than others think is safe. Dreaming more than others think is practical and expecting more than others think is possible.*
—Anonymous

*And I believe that it is in you to be good citizens. And what is it to be a good citizen? It is to acknowledge the other person's rights before asserting your own, but always to be conscious of your own. It is to be free in thought and deed, but it is also to know that your freedom is subject to the other person's freedom. It is to create the useful and the beautiful with your own hands, and to admire what others have created in love and with faith.*
*It is to produce wealth by labor and only by labor, and to spend less than you have produced that your children may not be dependent on the state for support when you are no more. It is to stand before the towers of New York, Washington, Chicago and San Francisco saying in your heart, "I am the descendant of a people that built Damascus, and Biblus, and Tyre and Sidon, and Antioch, and now I am here to build with you, and with a will." It is to be proud of being an American, but it is also to be proud that your fathers and mothers came from a land upon which God laid His gracious hand and raised His messengers.*
—Khalil Gibran, 1926

This quote, part of a poem dedicated and entitled, "To Young Americans of Syrian Origin," summarizes the Arab-American community and its experience. I am tremendously moved and emotionally affected each time I read it. I am here to build with you…and with a will.

*The three C's for life are Communication, Compassion, and Compromise.*
—Zayada Shora

I quoted my mother several times in this book, and for good reason. Like her mother before her, she is full of practical wisdom. Her quotes about Islam, culture, and life have always been a guide for my life.

*Wise men speak because they have something to say. Fools because they have to say something.*
   —Plato

# Resources

**Islam:**

*Acts of Faith: The Story of an American Muslim, the Struggle for the Soul of a Generation*, by Eboo Patel.

*Covering Islam: How the Media and the Experts Determine How We See the Rest of the World*, by Edward Said.

*Islam: A Short History*, by Karen Armstrong.

*Jihad: The Trail of Political Islam*, by Gilles Kepel.

*Muslims in American History, A Forgotten Legacy*, by Jerald F. Dirks.

*Peace Be upon You, The Story of Muslim, Christian and Jewish Coexistence*, by Zachary Karabell.

*The Koran*, Edited by N.J. Dawood.*

*It must be noted that the *Quran* was born into the Arabic language the same way the *Bible* was in Aramaic. No one wholly understands everything in it and it is beyond anyone to truly "translate" what God's words mean. This is at best an interpretation. Additionally, Arabic is a far more complex language than English and thus translation becomes more difficult. If one were to truly grasp The Quran, they would need to read it and understand it in Arabic.

*Misquoting Muhammad*, by Jonathan A.C. Brown

*Covering Islam*, by Edward Said

*Homegrown: ISIS in America*, by Alexander Meleagrou-Hitchens, Seamus Hughes, and Bennet Clifford

*The Last Girl, My Story of Captivity, and My Fight Against the Islamic State*, by Nadia Murad

*Enemies Near and Far: How Jihadist Groups Strategize, Plot, and Learn*, by Daveed Gartenstein-Ross

*Black Flags, The Rise of ISIS*, by Joby Warrick

*Lost History: The Enduring Legacy of Muslim Scientists, Thinkers, and Artists*, by Michael H. Morgan.

*Unholy War: Terror in the Name of Islam*, by John Esposito.

*What Everyone Needs to Know About Islam*, by John Esposito.

**Arabs:**

*The Arabs,* by Eugene Rogan

*The Muqaddimah: An Introduction to History,* by Ibn Khaldun

*The New Arabs: How the Millennial Generation is Changing the Middle East,* by Juan Cole

*A Woman in the Crossfire; Diaries of the Syrian Revolution,* by Samar Yazbek

*The Crusades Through Arab Eyes,* by Amin Maalouf

*A History of Modern Morocco,* by Susan Gilson Miller

*Arab Voices Speak to American Hearts,* by Samar Dahmash-Jarrah.

*Guilty: Hollywood's Verdict on Arabs After 9/11,* by Jack G. Shaheen.

*Orientalism,* by Edward Said.

*The House of Wisdom: How the Arabs Transformed Western Civilization,* by Jonathan Lyons.

*The Prophet,* by Kahlil Gibran.

*Reel Bad Arabs: How Hollywood Vilifies a People,* by Jack G. Shaheen.

**Videos:**

*A Dream in Doubt*

*Reel Bad Arabs*

*Secrets of the Koran*

*When the World Spoke Arabic: The Golden Age of Arab Civilization*

# Notes

1. Barlow, Elizabeth, ed., *Evaluation of Secondary-Level Textbooks for Coverage of the Middle East and North Africa*, Center for Middle Eastern and North African Studies, Ann Arbor, MI; Middle East Studies Association, Tucson, AZ, 3rd edition, 1994.

2. *Id.*

3. "We the People of Arab Ancestry," US Census Bureau, March 2005. (Note: Although the census found an estimated 1.2 million Americans of Arab ancestry, those numbers are believed to be widely underrated and the three million population is a more accepted estimate.)

4. *Id.*

5. *CIA World Factbook*, Afghanistan, http://www.cia.gov/cia/publications/factbook/geos/af.html.

6. *Id.*

7. *Id.*

8. "Saudi Aramco World: The Arabs of Honduras," http://www.saudiaramcoworld.com/issue/200104/the.arabs.of.honduras.html.

9. *Id.*

10. *Id.*

11. "Wahhabi," *The Columbia Encyclopedia,* 6th ed., Columbia University Press, New York, 2001–04, www.bartleby.com/65/.

12. http://i-cias.com/e.o/sharia.html.

13. *The Holy Quran*, (111:7).

14. *Id*, (9:5).

15. *Id*, (5:32).

16. From a Hadith of the Prophet Muhammed. Terrorism, Al Muhaddith, http://www.muhaddith.org/Islam_Answers/Terrorism.html.

17. "Jesus and Mary in the Quran," http://www.submission.org/jesus/Mary-Jesus.html.

18. *The Holy Quran*, (2:62).

19. *Id*, (4:1).

20. "The Koran's Spirit of Gender Equality," http://www.qantara.de/webcom/show_article.php/_c-307/_nr-19/_p-1/i.html.

21. *The Holy Quran*, (4:32).

22. *Id*, (3:195).

23. Armstrong, Karen, "The Eve of Destruction," http://www.countercurrents.org/armstrong150204.htm.

24. *Arab Culture and Society*, American-Arab Anti-Discrimination Committee, http://www.adc.org/index.php?id=1172.

25. Armstrong, Karen, "The Eve of Destruction," *Guardian Unlimited*, January 15, 2004.

26. *Id*.

27. *Id*.

28. *The Holy Quran*, (4:3).

29. CIA World Factbook.

30. *Id*.

31. www.usinfo.state.gov.

32. CIA World Factbook, 2004.

33. *Id*.

34. "Facts about Arabs and the Arab World," American-Arab Anti-Discrimination Committee.

35. http://www.aneki.com/muslim.html.

36. Sikh American Legal Defense and Education Fund, www.saldef.org.

37. http://en.wikipedia.org/wiki/Bedouin.

38. US Census Bureau, Census 2000, Summary File 4.

39. "Demographic portrait of Muslim Americans", July 26, 2017

40. *Id*.

41. Belt, Don, "The World of Islam," *National Geographic*, January 2002, p. 85.

42. http://perresearch.org/pubs/483/muslim-americans.

43. Oversight of the Federal Bureau of Investigation, Statement for the Record, Christopher Wray, Director.

44. Cooper, Barry, *Unholy Terror: The Origin and Significance of Contemporary, Religion-based Terrorism*, March 2002.

45. "Jewish militant faces bomb trial," June 15, 2004, BBC News.

46. "Hindu hardliners 'led Gujarat attacks'," March 6, 2002, BBC News.

47. "Armed guards for Sri Lanka church," January 27, 2004, BBC News.

48. "Understanding Islam," Interview with Karen Armstrong, *Newsweek*, October 29, 2001.

49. Khawaja, Sobat, ed., "Islam: The Moral Code Re-Examined," www.proislam.com, March, 3, 2003.

50. *Id.*

51. Nawwab, Ismail I.; Speers, Peter C.; and Hoye, Paul F., eds, *ARAMCO and Its World: Arabia And The Middle East*, edited by, Islam and Islamic History Section, Arabian American Oil Company, Washington, DC, 1980.

52. M Erhayiem, http://www.arabicnumerals.cwc.net/.

53. http://www.fact-index.com/a/al/al_khwarizmi.html.

54. http://www.arab2.com/articles/a/A-is-for-Arabs-George-Rafael.html.

55. *Id.*

56. *Id.*

57. *Id.*

58. *Id.*

59. *Id.*

60. *Id.*

61. *Id.*

62. *Id.*

63. *Id.*

64. *Id.*

65. *Id.*

66. http://www.mediamonitors.net/sherri24.html.

67. *Id.*

68. *Id.*

69. *Id.*

70. *Id.*

71. "The impact of the Arab Culture on European Renaissance," http://www.isesco.org.ma/pub/Eng/Arabiculture/page4.html.

72. *USA Today*, cover story, April 20, 1995, p. 1 A.

73. ADC 1995 Report on Anti-Arab Racism.

74. *Chicago Tribune*, April 25, 1995, p. 20.

75. *Id.*

76. Shaheen, Jack G., *Reel Bad Arabs*, 2001, p. 51.

77. *Id.*

78. *Id.*

79. Waxman, Sharon, *The Washington Post*, November 6, 1998, p. 1.

80. Hoffman II, Michael, *Hoffman Wire*, Associated Press, May 14, 1999.

81. *Id.*

82. "Muslims are a growing presence in U.S., but still face negative views from the public" Pew Research Center, September 1, 2021.

83. Star Wars, Episode I – Yoda quote.

84. Whitney v. California, *274 US 357 (1927)*.

85. Waffle Classic - The Original Ice Cream Cone.

86. http://en.wikipedia.org/wiki/Mizrahi_Jews.

87. Royal Embassy of Saudi Arabia website, Traditional Dress and Jewelry.

88. http://inventory.overture.com/d/searchinventory/suggestion/,asof June 2005.

89. *Id.*

90. *Id.*

91. "We the People of Arab Ancestry," US Census Bureau, March 2005. (Note: Although the census found an estimated 1.2 million Americans of Arab ancestry, those numbers are believed to be widely underrated and the three million population is a more accepted estimate.)

92. "National Arab American Demographics", Arab American Institute 88.

93. El-Badry, Samia, "Arab-Americans are Well-Educated, Diverse, Affluent & Highly Entrepreneurial,"

94. *Arab-American Business*, November 2001.

95. *Id.*

96. *Id.*

97. *Id.*

98. Demographics, Arab American Institute Foundation, census-counts.org

99. "We the People of Arab Ancestry," p. 3.

100. *Id.*

101. *Id.*

102. *Id.*

103. *Id.*

104. *Id.*

105. *Id.*

106. *Id.*

107. *Id.*

108. *Id.*

109. *Id.*

110. *Id.*

111. *Id.*

112. "Arab-Americans are Well-Educated, Diverse, Affluent & Highly Entrepreneurial," www.arabamericanbusiness.com/ issue1_nov2001/sr_badry.html.

113. *Id.*

114. *Id.*

115. *Id.*

116. "We the People of Arab Ancestry," p. 11.

117. *Id.*

118. "Arab-Americans are Well-Educated, Diverse, Affluent & Highly Entrepreneurial," www.arabamericanbusiness.com/ issue1_nov2001/sr_badry.html.

119. "We the People of Arab Ancestry," p. 12.

120. *Id.*

121. "Arab-Americans are Well-Educated, Diverse, Affluent & Highly Entrepreneurial," www.arabamericanbusiness.com/issue1_nov2001/sr_badry.html.

122. *Id.*

123. *Id.*

124. "We the People of Arab Ancestry," p. 15.

125. *Id.*

126. El-Badry, Samia and Shabbas, Audrey, *Arab World Studies Notebook*, Middle East Policy Council, The Arab-Americans.

127. *Id.*

128. *Id.*

129. *Id.*

130. *Id.*

131. *Id.*

132. *Id.*

133. Samhan, Helen Hatab, "New Census Figures Show Continued Growth of the Arab-American Community," *Arab-American Business*. July 2002.

134. "Arab American Demographics," Arab American Institute. www.aaiusa.org/demographics.html.

135. McIntosh, Phyllis, "Islamic Influence Runs Deep in American Culture," Washington File, August 24, 2004.

136. *Id.*

137. *Id.*

138. *Id.*

139. *Id.*

140. http://archives.cnn.com/2002/EDUCATION/11/20/geography.quiz/.

141. "Study: Geography Greek to young Americans," http://www.cnn.com, April 2006.

142. "Most Young Americans Can't Pass a Test on Global Affairs – Can You?" National Geographic, September 12, 2016.

143. *Webster's Deluxe Unabridged Dictionary*, Dorset & Baber, New York, 1983, http://www.adc.org/index.php?id=1172.

144. Erichsen, Gerald, *Spanish's Arab Connection*, http://spanish.about.com/cs/historyofspanish/a/arabicwords.html.

145. Clark, Yvonne, "Moors and Arabs," http://www.africawithin.com/moors/moors_and_arabs.html.

# Section Two

In the Reference section the reader will find resources to assist in mining the book as well as features designed to set our discussion into historical and geographic context.

# Contents (Section Two)

# Glossary

**Allah:** (See page 42)

**Al-Qaeda:** An international terroristic Sunni Islamic movement founded under the leadership of Osama bin Laden. Al-Qaeda terror groups have attacked civilian and military targets in various countries, the most notable being the September 11, 2001 attacks on New York's World Trade Center, the Pentagon, and Shanksville, Pennsylvania. In response the US government launched a military and intelligence campaign against Al-Qaeda. Its central effort involved a war in Afghanistan to destroy Al-Qaeda's bases there and overthrow the Taliban, the country's Muslim fanatical rulers who harbored bin Laden and his followers. "Al-Qaeda" is Arabic for "The Base," referring to a database of followers.

Al-Qaeda terror techniques include suicide attacks and simultaneous bombings of different targets. These activities may involve members of the organization, who have taken a pledge of loyalty to bin Laden, or the much more numerous "Al-Qaeda-linked" individuals who have undergone training in one of its camps in Afghanistan or Sudan. Al-Qaeda's objectives include the end of foreign influence in Muslim countries and the creation of a new Islamic caliphate. Reported beliefs include that a Christian-Jewish alliance is conspiring to destroy Islam and that the killing of bystanders and civilians is Islamically justified in holy war. Its management philosophy has been described as "centralization of decision and decentralization of execution."

Al-Qaeda grew out of the Services Office, a clearinghouse for the international Muslim brigade opposed to the 1979 Soviet invasion of Afghanistan. In the 1980s, the Services Office—run by bin Laden and the Palestinian religious scholar Abdullah Azzam—recruited, trained, and financed thousands of foreign mujahadeen, or holy warriors, from more than fifty countries. Bin Laden wanted these fighters to continue the "holy war" beyond Afghanistan. He formed Al-Qaeda circa 1988.

Noting Al-Qaeda's diffuse nature, the July 19, 2008, issue of the Economist wrote: "Its core members may number only hundreds, but it has connections of all kinds to military groups with thousands or even tens of thousands of fighters. Al-Qaeda is a terrorist organization, a militant network, and a subculture of rebellion all at the same time." It continues: "Some [experts] describe it as a venture-capital firm that invests in promising terrorist projects. Others speak of it as a global 'brand' maintained by its leaders through their propaganda, with its growing number of 'franchises' carrying out attacks."

**Arabic:** The language of Arabs and Islam, included here because the differences between Arabic and English demonstrate the extreme differences between Arab and American societies. To the English-speaker Arabic sounds different, looks different, reads different. Arabic uses an entirely different script. That script is read from right to left, the reverse of our way, and books are read from what we would call back to front. In addition, the styles of expression of the two languages differ. Arabic is not easily translated and therefore the beauty and impact of the *Quran* are lost on people who read it in translation.

Classified as Central Semitic, Arabic is closely related to Hebrew and Aramaic and has its roots in a Proto-Semitic common ancestor. Modern Arabic is classified as a macro-language with 27 sub-languages spoken throughout the Arab world. Standard Arabic is widely studied and known throughout the Islamic world.

During the Middle Ages, Arabic was a major vehicle of culture, especially in science, mathematics and philosophy, with the result that European languages have borrowed numerous words from it. These include algebra, alcohol, alchemy, alkali, zenith, sugar, cotton and magazine.

**Beheading:** Islam in the time of Mohammad adopted many practices that were traditional to the Arab tribes of the day. Beheading enemies was a widely used form of execution in the era when Islam was being established. It's possible, given the modes of execution at that time, that beheading was one of the more enlightened and humane forms of it.

The modern-day beheadings, photographed for television, are clearly designed to terrorize opponents. The intention seems un-Islamic.

**Caliph:** The now-defunct title meaning the head of state in a caliphate (a territory governed by Muslims). Today, there is no global umma. It is false to treat the Muslim community as one monolith. This title designated the leader of the Islamic umma, an Islamic community ruled by Sharia law. The successors to Mohammad were called caliphs. After the first four caliphs (Abu Bakr, Umar, Uthman, and Ali), the title was claimed by succeeding dynasties: the Umayyads, the Abbasids, and the Ottomans. Most historical Muslim governors were called sultans or emirs, and gave allegiance to a caliph, but at times had very little real authority.

**Chador:** An outer garment or open cloak worn by some Muslim women in Iran and Pakistan. This is often an expansion on an attempt to be modest in Islam. Other Muslim women may choose to wear variations such as the abaya or in Afghanistan the burka. It consists of a full-length semi-circle of fabric open down the front, thrown over the head and held shut in front. These clothes are meant to support modesty—required of both women and men, but it is supposed to be a woman's choice as to how to express such modesty. A chador has no hand openings or closures but is held shut by the hands or by wrapping the ends around the waist. This is different from the simple veil that some Muslim women wear.

**Change:** We often ask: Why are Arab and/or Muslim societies so resistant to change? In considering this question, perhaps it's well to point out that 800 years ago, when Muslim civilization was at its height, that civilization was both the product of change and its engine in science and technology. In addition, Arab societies underwent extensive urbanization in the 20th century.

But it may also be useful to look at recent change in American society. Americans are accustomed to change; it's a fact of life in their culture. Change, innovation, originality of thought and diversity are all regarded as American values. Moreover, America's political system institutionalizes at least the possibility of change every four years.

In addition, the 20th century has been an era of unparalleled technological change in the West, beginning with movies, automobiles and telephones, moving through airplanes, television, space exploration and sophisticated weaponry to the internet. Due to these developments, the world for Americans has shrunk incredibly in size, speaking metaphorically. A society comfortable with change can accommodate these technological advances. There have also been extraordinary cultural changes: the extension of women's rights, civil rights and the greater acceptance of alternative lifestyles. The fluidity of migration has also caused changes in the US. People have not always adjusted easily to these changes as the rise of fundamentalism in America attests.

By contrast change and originality of thought are not as viable in present-day Islamic societies. The general political system in the Arab or Muslim worlds is strong man rule, well exemplified by Saddam Hussein. Dictatorships discourage change unless it is instituted by the regime. (The Shah of Iran discovered that change can develop a momentum of its own and lead to the overthrow of a regime.) At the beginning of the 20th century Arabs were ruled by the decadent Ottoman Empire, by tribal leaders (ibn Saud) or by English or French colonial regimes. None of these encouraged change. Moreover, adherence to tradition and the espousing of a social system and set of laws enunciated more than a thousand years earlier have impeded change.

While the Islamic empire responded successfully to change in previous centuries, it now finds itself very far behind a West that seems to it magnificent in power while being decadent in culture. How to contend with – and emerge from – this situation has been a perplexing question for both Muslims and the West. Some Arabs have questioned the relevance of Quranic teachings. Muslim fundamentalists have embraced them unreservedly, wishing to force their societies to return to a pure and purely Islamic way of life. This will require overturning governments in their own countries. Some fundamentalists see attacking the West as a first step in the process of doing this.

**Crusades:** A series of military expeditions waged by much of feudal Christian Europe with the goal of recapturing Jerusalem and the Holy Land from Muslim rule. They are seen by some as a flip side of the civilization conflict launched by Muslim extremists against the West most notably by the attacks of 9/11. During Europe's Middle Ages, Muslim civilization, although beset by rivalries, led the world in scientific discoveries and technological domination and was at the height of its influence.

Since the 8th century devout Christians had been making pilgrimages to the Holy Sepulcher, the tomb in Jerusalem where Jesus was supposed to have been laid to rest. The crusades were undertaken to permit Christians to continue making pilgrimages to holy sites by retrieving them from Muslim rule. They took place over a period of the two centuries, from 1095 to 1291.

The crusades were actually triggered by a call from the Christian Eastern Orthodox Byzantine Empire for help against the expansion of the Muslim Seljuk Turks into Anatolia (central Turkey). While ostensibly religiously motivated and sanctioned by the Pope, Christendom's supreme ruler at the time, they inspired masses of Europeans, some in armies, others as pilgrim adventurers, to wander across southeastern Europe, through Constantinople (now Istanbul which was sacked in 1204) and into Asia Minor. They succeeded in recapturing Jerusalem only to lose it to the brilliant and honorable Muslim general Saladin. The crusades spurred the transformation of Europe out of feudalism, but failed in terms of basic goals. Besides Saladin, crusaders best known to Americans are the English king Richard the Lion-Hearted and Francis of Assisi, later a saint.

The crusades, seen as an all-out Western attack on Muslim civilization, still provoke excited and hostile reactions among Muslims. The word itself can act as a red flag to some.

**Cutting the hands of thieves:** As a matter of sharia law (remember, Sharia law is simply religious law as with other faiths), in accordance with the *Quran* and several hadith, theft is punished by imprisonment or amputation of hands or feet, depending on the number of times theft was committed and on the items stolen. Before the punishment is executed eyewitnesses must say under oath that they saw the person stealing. Without witnesses the punishment cannot be executed. Other requirements specify that the thief must be adult and sane and that the theft was not caused by hunger, necessity or duress. If the thief repents, the punishment is not imposed. As a result, the actual instances of hands being amputated are relatively few.

**Fatwa:** (pl. *fatawa*) A ruling on Islamic law issued by an Islamic scholar, essentially a religious declaration. Contrary to what some believe, it is not a "death order". In theory, to be valid, a *fatwa* must be in line with relevant legal proofs, deduced from Quranic verses and *hadiths*; issued by a person (or a board) having due knowledge and sincerity of heart; be free from individual opportunism, and not depending on political servitude; and be adequate with the needs of the contemporary world. Today, *Fatawa* do not always meet these criteria.

The obligation of individual Muslims in relation to them varies from place to place, from circumstance to circumstance. Scholar of religion Karen Armstrong reports, for example, that 44 out of 45 member states attending a meeting of the Islamic Congress condemned the fatwa of Iran's Ayatollah Khomeini against Salmon Rushdie as un-Islamic.

**Female circumcision/female genital mutilation/female genital cutting:** The excision or tissue removal of any part of the female genitalia for cultural, religious or other non-medical reasons.

Writes scholar of religion Karen Armstrong: "Feminists frequently condemn 'Islam' for the custom of female circumcision. This despite the fact that it is really an African practice, is never mentioned in the [*Quran*], is not prescribed by three of the four main schools of Islamic jurisprudence, and was absorbed into the fourth school in North Africa where it was a fact of life."

**Fundamentalism:** In recent years "fundamentalism" has come to refer to strong adherence to a set of conservative and traditional beliefs and practices, perhaps especially when the values they espouse have come under attack. Those values relate particularly to cultural or religious practices and appear to challenge the adherent's sense of identity.

The term "fundamentalism" originally referred to a set of beliefs—regarded as "religious fundamentals"—within the American Protestant community early in the 20th century. Their values were being challenged by modernism.

Fundamentalism is seen as a basically religious response to change and the strains it causes. Given the kind of change the world has experienced in the past 100 years (see "Change" above), it is not surprising that evidences of fundamentalism have sprung up around the world. In the US there are both Catholic fundamentalism and the Protestant variety. American fundamentalists are particular opponents of cultural change as represented by the now familiar sexual revolution, the abortion it condones, pressures to accept homosexual life-styles and immigration.

Islamic fundamentalists feel rage and humiliation at the power and arrogance of the West, its military and economic power, its overwhelming cultural imports, and its colonial and post-colonial encroachments on their territory. They have felt lost and disoriented by their own political impotence and the secular lifestyle invasions of the West. Revolted by the future offered by the secular and impious West, disgusted by the seeming stasis of the present, Muslim fundamentalists pin their hopes on a restoration of the golden age of Islamic flowering at the time of Mohammad and his immediate successors thirteen hundred years ago. This strikes most Westerners as extreme folly, given the change that the world has experienced in the interim.

But how the West can help Muslims to find an accommodation with the modern world that works for them has so far eluded it. The West's lack of cultural sensitivity and curiosity, its hubris and its incompetence in waging both war and peace have immensely complicated the attempt.

Arab-American educator Audrey Shabbas offers a different perspective. She writes: "The Western term 'Fundamentalism' does not accurately describe the modern movement in Islamic countries to renew Islamic values in Muslim personal and public life. Muslims prefer the term 'revivalism' as a more accurate description of this renewal, whose manifestations include an increase in religious observance (mosque attendance, Ramadan fast, wearing traditional Islamic dress); revitalization of mystical orders; the growth of numerous religious publications and media programming; support for the implementation of Islamic law; and the growth and creation of Islamic organizations and movements."

**Hadith:** Oral traditions relating to the words and deeds of Mohammad. *Hadith* collections are regarded as important tools for determining the *Sunnah*, or Muslim way of life, by all traditional schools of the Islamic legal system.

**Hajj:** An ancient Arab ritual involving a pilgrimage to Mecca and its shrine, the Ka'aba, the heart of Islam. The *hajj* predates Islam and was considered ancient even in the time of Mohammad the Prophet. The Ka'aba was believed to have been built by Abraham and his son Ishmael, the father of the Arabs. A sanctuary surrounds Mecca in which no violence was to occur even in the days when Arabia was inhabited by contending nomadic tribes.

The *hajj* is one of the five pillars (requirements) of Islam. It involves making a pilgrimage to Mecca in order to perform a series of rituals. At the Ka'aba the pilgrim walks counter-clockwise around the cube-shaped building in the center of *Masjid Al Haram* mosque toward which all Muslims orient their prayers as Mohammad and millions of other pilgrims have done. The pilgrim walks or runs between the hills of Al-Safa and Al-Marwah (as the abandoned Hagar, Ishmael's mother, is thought to have done in seeking water for her son). The pilgrim stands in vigil on the plains of Mount Arafat, drinks from the Zamzam well (which sprang forth, according to legend, when Ishmael stamped his foot) and gathers pebbles at Muzdalifah and throws them at pillars at Mina in order to "stone the devil."

During the *hajj* male pilgrims wear a garment of two sheets of unhemmed cloth as Mohammad himself did when in 632 he led exclusively his Muslim followers on a *hajj* from Medina. This clothing demonstrates the equality of all pilgrims before God. After performing *hajj* rituals the pilgrims cut their hair, sacrifice an animal in order to feed the poor and celebrate the festival of *Eid ul-Adha.*

In recent years *hajj* pilgrims have numbered an estimated two million. Due to the multitudes some rituals have become stylized. Pebbles are now thrown at walls with catch-bins. Despite crowd-control techniques, pilgrims are still trampled in the crush and ramps occasionally fall due to the weight of pilgrims, causing deaths.

**Harem:** The women's section in a polygamous household. There women's quarters are enclosed and forbidden to men. An Arab *harem* does not necessarily consist solely of women with whom the head of the household has sexual relations (wives and concubines). It may also include their young offspring, female relatives and other women. A *harem* may be a palatial complex, as in romantic tales, in which case it includes staff (women and eunuchs). Or it may simply be women's quarters, in the Ottoman tradition (*harem* comes from the Turkish) separated from the men's *selamlik*, that portion of a Turkish house reserved for men. This practice no longer exists in today's Arab world except for a few scattered examples in select societies.

**Hijab:** In Western usage *hijab* usually refers to the headscarf worn by Muslim women to cover their hair and ears. In Islamic scholarship *hijab* denotes morality encouraged by modesty.

In Western countries wearing the *hijab* scarf serves not only as an act of respect to Muslim tradition, but also as a woman's way of declaring her identity as a Muslim and her solidarity with other Muslims. Because of this, Muslim girls (and also Sikh boys) in France were prohibited from wearing head coverings to school as a means of protecting the state school's secularist values.

Wearing the *hijab* is intended to be the woman's choice to cover up with the veil. Modesty is expected of both men and women.

**Honor killing:** The murder of a family member (almost always a woman) by a male relative in order to erase a real or perceived humiliation of the family as a result of the victim's behavior. The offensive behavior is usually sexual, sometimes immodesty, sometimes disapproved liaisons. Honor killings sometimes occur among Muslim tribes in Arab countries and Pakistan, some among Kurds and Sikhs.

An Amnesty International statement declares: "The regime of honor is unforgiving: women on whom suspicion has fallen are not given an opportunity to defend themselves, and family members have no socially acceptable alternative but to remove the stain on their honor by attacking the woman." The United Nations Population Fund estimates that worldwide honor-killing victims may number as high as 5,000 women each year.

Islamic religious authorities claim that extra-legal punishments such as honor killings are prohibited. They cite the killings as a pre-Islamic cultural practice which continues to shape Muslim actions. They contend that murderers of females use Islam to justify honor killing, but they claim that there is no support for the act in the religion itself.

**Jihad:** (See page 45)

**Ka'aba:** A shrine venerated from time immemorial, considered by Muslims to be the most sacred spot on earth around which has been built the Great Mosque of Mecca. Muslims turn toward the shrine during prayer as the symbolic house of God. They are encouraged to visit and walk around it seven times in the *hajj* pilgrimage, one of the five pillars of Islam. The Ka'aba is cube-shaped, constructed of gray stone and marble, its corners corresponding roughly to the points of the compass. During most of the year an enormous black cloth covers the Ka'aba, ornamented with Quranic sayings woven in gold.

Karen Armstrong's biography *Mohammad* offers this account by the Iranian philosopher Ali Shariati of the experience of circumambulating (walking around) the Ka'aba: "As you circumambulate and move closer to the Ka'aba, you feel like a small stream merging with a big river. Carried by a wave you lose touch with the ground. Suddenly, you are floating, carried on by the flood. As you approach the center, the pressure of the crowd squeezes you so hard that you are given a new life. You are now part of the People; you are now a Man, alive and eternal…"

**Madrassa education:** The Arabic word for any type of school, secular or religious, is *madrassa*. In common English usage the word has been taken to mean a school giving Islamic religious instruction.

Islamic schools typically offer two courses of study: memorization of the *Quran* (which is shorter than the *Bible's* New Testament) and preparation to become an accepted scholar in the community. Students study Arabic, *Quran* interpretation, *sharia* law, *hadith*, logic and Muslim history. More advanced *madrassas* offer world history, science, English and foreign languages.

The concern about *madrassas* in the United States has been two-fold: first, how can Islamic education, predominant in the Arab world, prepare young Muslims to interface with a complicated world? Second, if some *madrassas* are fashioning Muslim fundamentalists, are they also training young men to be violent extremists and, if so, what can be done about it?

During the Afghan resistance against the Soviets Saudi Arabia financed the establishment of *madrassas* in Pakistan. Those *madrassas* teach the austere and rigid form of Islam called *Wahhabism*; they educated many Taliban. This did not concern Americans when the fundamentalists were fighting the Soviets. But today the fundamentalists are fighting against America—as a reconstituted Taliban in Afghanistan and as violent extremists in Iraq. Some observers say that an education in *Quran*-by-rote does not equip a person for the technical and linguistic skills a terrorist needs. Even so, say others, the training of fundamentalists with mistaken, prejudiced and uneducated ideas about the world and the West should concern Americans.

**Mecca:** The holiest city of Islam, site of the Ka'aba, a shrine which, legend says, was built by Abraham and his son Ishmael, father of the Arabs. The shrine is located at the Zamzam spring, the water source that created an oasis at Mecca. Situated between mountains, the city hosts an estimated two million Muslim *hajj* pilgrims each year; they visit the sacred mosque and perform rituals comprising one of the five pillars of Islam. People from other faiths are prohibited from entering the city.

**Modesty of dress:** Modesty of dress is expected of all Muslims, both male and female.

Moreover, clothing should not reveal body contours nor should it be eye-catching. Some Western Muslim women who dress in accordance with these requirements stress that they feel freedom, not confinement, inside Islamic dress. There are various interpretations of what modesty requires. Some Western Muslim women wear the headscarf; others dress in conventional Western styles.

The *Quran* states: "Say to the believing men and women that they should lower their gaze and guard their modesty: that will make for greater purity for them: And God is well acquainted with all that they do." [24:30]

Given this tradition of modesty and the general seclusion of most Muslim women, one can understand how American movies with their frequent nudity or near-nudity and their depiction of sex acts give offense to devout Muslims and are regarded by some as evidence of a decadent society.

**Mohammad:** One of history's extraordinary men, 570-632 CE.

Says the Encyclopedia Brittanica: "Founder of the religion of Islam and of the Arab Empire, initiator of religious, social and cultural developments of monumental significance in the history of mankind." Says Wikipedia: "the founder of Islam regarded by Muslims as the last messenger and prophet of God (Allah in Arabic). Muslims do not believe that he was the creator of a new religion, but the restorer of the original, uncorrupted monotheistic faith of Adam, Abraham and others. They see him as the last and the greatest in a series of prophets." Says scholar of religions Karen Armstrong: "a complex, passionate man who sometimes did things that it is difficult for us [in the West] to accept, but who had genius of a profound order and founded a religion and a cultural tradition that was not based on the sword – despite Western myth – and whose name 'Islam' signifies peace and reconciliation."

Mohammad lived at a time when Arab tribes were leaving their traditional nomadic way of life on the steppes and settling into towns. A married merchant resident in Mecca, Mohammad began to receive revelations at age 40. While on a religious retreat in the mountains outside Mecca, Mohammad was visited by an angel who told him, "Recite." Mohammad at first refused, but was so overwhelmed by the angel that he eventually began to verbalize messages that became the basis of the *Quran*, Islam's holy book. (Mohammad was probably illiterate. The recitations were later transcribed. The Arabic *Quran* (*Qu'ran*) means the Recitation.) When Mohammad continued to receive the revelations—the main message of which was that there was one only God—he began to share them first with his wife, then with clan members and eventually with his tribal brothers, the Quraysh who had been settled in Mecca, taking up a life as traders, for about two generations.

Although Mohammad's call for worshipping only one God brought him followers, it also caused him and his followers great difficulties with the powerful clans of the Quraysh. They were not ready to renounce the pagan gods of their fathers. The tensions and harassment of Muslims became so extreme that a large portion of the followers went to live in Abyssinia (now Ethiopia) in 616.

When the harassment continued, it became clear that Mohammad and his followers must look for another place to live. Just at this time two Arab tribes had settled in the oasis of Yathrib, north of Mecca, where Jewish immigrants were farming. Rivalry between the groups meant that they needed an outsider to mediate between them. Accustomed to the monotheism of their Jewish neighbors, the now settled tribes of Yathrib accepted Mohammad as their change agent.

Mohammad and his people thus took a significant modernizing step. They cut themselves off from the system of protection based on blood ties, a paramount value among the Arabs, trusting that those who agreed to protect and help them, known as the *Ansar*, would in fact do this. Mohammad's transfer to Medina in 622 CE—also termed his "flight" there—marks the beginning of the Muslim era and is called the *hejra*.

When the Quraysh of Mecca realized that Mohammad's people had been leaving in small groups, the tribal leaders decided that Mohammed, who waited behind in Mecca until all his people had gone, should be killed. A group of young men, one from each clan, thus avoiding a blood feud, was appointed to do the deed. But Mohammad escaped.

En route to Medina he and a companion (Abu Bakr, who later succeeded him as the first *caliph*) hid in a cave. One of the great stories of God's protection concerns this cave. When the Quraysh pursued Mohammad, who remained in the cave with Abu Bakr, they found a spider's web covering it as well as an acacia tree in front of it, with a rock-dove nesting in it sitting on her eggs.

Since his followers had no way of sustaining themselves at Medina, Mohammad instructed them to raid Quraysh caravans passing nearby. Learning that Mohammad intended to stage a caravan ambush at a place called Badr, the Quraysh sent out an army to liquidate him. But Mohammad's men won a seemingly miraculous victory, seen as divine intervention, a *furqan* or sign of salvation. Muslims liken this event to the escape by Moses and the Children of Israel from the Egyptians at the miraculous parting of the Red Sea.

Two years later, in 625, however, the Quraysh, intent on vengeance, massed for an attack on Medina. Although Mohammad had great difficult rallying a unified force, his men met the Quraysh at Uhud, outside Medina. They were defeated. Trying to rally his retreating men, Mohammad was hit on the head. Supposing him dead, the Quraysh withdrew. Only stunned, Mohammad was able to regroup his men and chase the Quraysh back toward Mecca for three days. The defeat at Uhud, however, left the Muslims deeply discouraged and depressed.

In 627 the Quraysh again sought to rid themselves of Mohammad by taking the attack into Medina itself. Mohammad led his followers to build a series of trenches at places where the Quraysh might gain entry to the settlement. The trenches, which his adversaries had never seen before, thwarted attempts by horses and camels in enter Medina. The Quraysh besieged Medina. They had, moreover, begun to negotiate with a Jewish tribe, resident at Medina, the Bani Qurayzah, for entry into the city. Distrust forestalled the triggering of this betrayal. Mohammad got wind of it and after three weeks of siege the Quraysh pulled out. Mohammad's victory at the Battle of the Trenches (for so it was regarded) made him the most powerful man in Arabia. The tribal ethic of the time forced him to deal harshly with the traitorous Bani Qurayzah.

While the victory solved Mohammad's security problem, he was trying to build a new kind of society based on his revelations. This meant that the next challenge with the Quraysh was to achieve reconciliation. In early 628 Mohammad decided to subscribe to ancient Arab practice and lead a *hajj* to the Ka'aba, the holiest of Arab shrines, in the Quraysh city of Mecca. About a thousand supporters accompanied him. They wore the traditional garb of Arab pilgrims, two pieces of cloth draped one about the shoulders, the other about the waist, and carried no weapons. A sanctuary surrounding Mecca prohibited acts of violence.

By tradition, pilgrims were free to enter Mecca in safety. But the Quraysh refused to allow Mohammad and his people into the city. When they reached the edge of the sanctuary, however, tradition held that they could not be attacked. But would the Quraysh honor this tradition? In this dangerous situation Mohammad asked each of his followers to swear an oath of loyalty to him. Negotiations then began. Mohammad made concessions to the Quraysh with which many of his followers disagreed. But because they had sworn loyalty to Mohammed, he was able to retain their support. The treaty made at this time led to better relations with his old enemies.

Of this moment Karen Armstrong writes, "[Mohammad] had intuitively penetrated to a deeper understanding of the dynamics of change in Arabia, and events would vindicate his insight. From this point, now that he had saved the *umma* [his followers] from the threat of extinction, the *jihad* would become an effort of peace that demanded all his patience and ingenuity." Muslims speak of a "lesser *jihad*" (by which they mean warfare) and a "greater *jihad*" (which is the struggle for a better understanding of God and the building of a better society).

In 630 Mohammad returned to Mecca, vanquished pagan Quraysh who wished to fight and welcomed into Islam those who wished to be his followers. He smashed the pagan idols in the Ka'aba, consecrated it to God and issued a general amnesty. Within a few years pagan worship had ceased in Mecca.

As a result of his power, Mohammad was able to break the patterns of tribal alliances that had previously characterized Arabia. Increasingly nomadic tribes chose to ally themselves with him. They promised to renounce idolatry, furnish troops when needed, not to attack the *umma* and to pay the tithing and alms demanded of all Muslims as one of the five pillars of their faith.

Mohammad's exploits as a political leader can overshadow the significance of his greater work. This was the founding of a religion that grew dramatically after his death, demonstrating its validity to its converts; to encourage individual values and stress the individual's fate in a society that had been highly communal; to replace narrow tribal loyalties with those to the ever-growing *umma*; to create a community in Medina that served as an example to others and to codify in the *Quran* the precepts that had been revealed to him over the years.

**Muslim:** According to Arab-American educator Audrey Shabbas, "A Muslim is anyone who says publicly, 'There is no God but God, and Mohammad is the messenger of God.'" I would clarify, anyone who believes it, not just says it.

She continues, "The term 'Mohammedan' is offensive to Muslims and should not be used. Muslims worship God, not Mohammad, who warned his followers: "Do not exceed bounds in praising me as did the Christians in praising Jesus, the Son of Mary, by calling Him God, and the Son of God… I am only the Lord's servant: Then call me the servant of God and His messenger.'"

**Muslim Brotherhood:** Officially known as the Society of Muslim Brothers, the Muslim Brotherhood is a multi-national Sunni Islamist movement and the world's largest, most influential political Islamist group. Founded by the Sufi schoolteacher Hassan al-Banna in 1928, the Brotherhood is the largest political opposition organization in many Arab nations, particularly Egypt.

Organized by cells, the Brotherhood spread rapidly throughout the Muslim world, establishing schools, small-scale industries and clinics. A decade after its founding it became increasingly political, espousing a return to Islamic purity, the establishment of a unified Muslim state, and rejecting Westernization, secularization and modernization.

Its credo is: " God is our objective. The Prophet is our leader. *Quran* is our law. *Jihad* is our way. Dying in the way of God is our highest hope."

Officially disbanded after the 1952 coup during which Mohammad Naquib and Gamal Abdel Nasser overthrew the Egyptian monarchy, the Brotherhood went underground. In 1954 it was outlawed following student disturbances which it fomented. It survives, nonetheless, repeatedly challenging Arab or Muslim governments with violence and demonstrations and suffering oppression.

**Oppression of women in Islam:** A Muslim view of this matter is that in Islam—in principle, if not always in practice—women and men are equal. However, they do have different natures, biologically, psychologically and physiologically, and therefore different roles. A significant difference between the rights of Muslim women and American women, contend some Muslims, is the manner in which those rights were conferred. In the US women had to struggle for rights, such as voting, and had to prove their capacities by extraordinary service in wartime, for example, in factory work. Muslim women were given their rights by God through revelation to the Prophet and these cannot be changed.

Interestingly, in Islam women have always had rights to own property and to have inheritances. These rights came to Western women much later.

**Polygamy:** A widespread practice throughout the ages, seen generally in the form of polygyny (one man having several wives) and much more rarely in the form of polyandry (one woman with several husbands). Polygamy occurred in many traditional societies, on one hand, because tradition required that all women be under the protection of a man and, on the other, because plural wives were a way of manifesting a man's wealth, a kind of conspicuous consumption, in societies with few material possessions.

In traditional tribal societies, like that of Arab nomads, raiding caused the loss of men. Polygamy was a way of restoring protection to women. In societies that practiced levirate, Biblical Hebrews, for example, a man inherited his dead brother's widow(s) if she had no sons.

In Islam a man may have up to four wives except where monogamy is enforced by law, as in Turkey. The *Quran* specifically states that polygamous men must treat their wives fairly, housing them equally, spending equal amounts of time with and money on each woman. Men who cannot do this in good conscience are advised to avoid multiple wives.

Arab-American educator Audrey Shabbas writes: "Today, polygamy is illegal in many Arab countries... Several Arab countries permit polygamy under certain conditions such as the approval of the first wife, the approval of the judge, financial ability to support two wives, or a medical document certifying that the first wife cannot bear children. Today polygamous marriage represents less than 5% of all marriages and is rapidly disappearing as these countries become more developed and literate."

**Pre-Islamic past:** All religions rise out of a social context and help adherents deal with the problems posed by that context. Islam rose in the harsh and hostile environment of the Arabian steppes, among people who had left behind——for only about a century—a nomadic life. The harshness of the steppes meant that people could survive only by forming closely-knit groups, tribes made up clans, held together by kinship ties where the needs of the group were paramount and individualism had no place. These tribalists developed a highly masculine ethic based on – to quote Karen Armstrong—"courage in battle, patience and endurance in suffering, and a dedication to the chivalrous duties of avenging wrong done to the tribe." Women had no rights and were treated hardly better than animals. These people were polytheists. They did not believe in an afterlife, but observed rituals at shrines, the chief of which was the Ka'aba at Mecca.

There circumambulating (walking around) the Ka'aba had long been practiced in pre-Islamic times as Muslims do today in the *hajj*.

About 500 CE, a tribe called the Quraysh settled in Mecca, an oasis watered by the Zamzam well at the terminus of a caravan route. The Quraysh was comprised of some 14 clans, of which the Hashim, Mohammad's clan was in decline. Nomadic life had been strictly egalitarian. After the Quraysh settled in Mecca, however, people became more individualistic, more capitalistic, more concerned with material wealth, sacrificing concern for fellow tribesmen. As a result, the tribe's social fabric began to fray. Out of the tensions created, Islam arose.

**Prophets:** Prophets of Islam are male human beings who are regarded by Muslims to be prophets chosen by God. All prophets preached the same message: to believe in one God, forswear idolatry, follow God's word, refrain from sin. These prophets all came to preach Islam and to tell of the coming of the final prophet and messenger of God: the Prophet Mohammad.

Muslims believe the first prophet was Adam. Others include Nuh (Noah), Ibrahim (Abraham), Musa (Moses) and Isa (Jesus) who is, as in Christianity, the result of a virgin birth. The last prophet was Mohammad.

Muslims believe that God has sent over 124,000 messengers all over the world, but select few prophets of which Mohammad was the last.

Although Jesus fits the definition of a prophet ("a religious teacher or leader regarded as, or claiming to be, divinely inspired" *Webster's New World Dictionary*), Christians do not generally regard him as a prophet. In fact, the *Bible* says that "a messenger" (John the Baptist) was sent to preach the imminence of Jesus' arrival.

**Qibla:** An Arabic word for the direction of the Ka'aba in Mecca, the direction that should be faced when a Muslim prays. Most mosques contain a niche in a wall that indicates the *qibla*.

After emigrating to Medina, Mohammad and his followers faced in the direction of Jerusalem when praying, following the practice of the Jews. According to a tradition, Abraham abandoned Hagar and his son Ishmael, seen as the father of the Arabs, in the valley of Mecca. Later when he visited them, said the tradition, Abraham and Ishmael built the Ka'aba. One Friday while he was leading prayers (and facing toward Jerusalem), Mohammad received a revelation from God that henceforth he and his followers should pray facing the direction of the Ka'aba. Mohammad instructed his followers to face in that direction. They obeyed and have been doing so ever since.

The larger significance of this action is that Islam relinquished any dependency on the prophecies of earlier traditions and declared itself a religion.

**Quraysh:** The Arab tribe from which Mohammad descended. Formerly nomadic, the Quraysh, comprised of 14 clans, had been settled in the oasis of Mecca for about two generations at the time of Mohammad's revelations. When Mohammad began to preach Islam, the Quraysh rejected him. Mohammad was forced to battle them over most of a decade before achieving an accommodation with them.

***Quran:*** The holy book of Islam. It contains revelations to the Prophet Mohammad offering divine guidance and direction for mankind. Muslims regard the original text in Arabic, said to have indescribable beauty and impact, to be the word of God. They see the *Quran* as God's final revelation to mankind.

The word *Quran* (*Qu'ran* in Arabic) means "recitation." Mohammad recited these revelations through his interactions with the Angel Gabriel, which were memorized by his followers or written down on whatever material (bark, stone) was at hand.

The *Quran* has 114 chapters of varying lengths, each called a *sura*.

Translating the *Quran* in a way that suggests the power of the original has proved problematic. Since Arabic words can have a variety of meanings depending on context, accurate translation has been difficult.

The *Quran* can be read online. Check out the recommended resources section for a good translation.

**Qutb, Sayyid:** An influential Islamic fundamentalist and extremist thinker and a leading Muslim Brotherhood advocate in the 1950s and 1960s. Sayyid Qutb could recite the *Quran*, which he had memorized, at age ten. After a university education and a period as an Education Ministry functionary, Qutb spent about a year in the United States, becoming completely disenchanted with it.

Returning to his native Egypt, he became an influential figure in the Muslim Brotherhood. Following an attempt by members of the Brotherhood to assassinate Nasser, its leaders were jailed. Qutb was tortured. Later, however, he was given the freedom to write and produced an extensive commentary on the *Quran*. It won him a reputation as an important radical Islamist. In a manifesto called "Milestones" he wrote that "the Muslim community has been extinct for a few centuries." He wished to see its revival. Freed from jail for a short time, he was later rearrested and executed.

A notable disciple of Qutb is Ayman al-Zawahiri, who joined the Muslim Brotherhood at age 14 and is now Osama bin Laden's deputy in Al-Qaeda.

Qutb is included here because he did the same thing about America—hated it without understanding it—that we hope readers of this book will not do in judging Muslims, Arabs and Arab-Americans. Qutb visited in the United States for a bit more than a year (1948-1950).

In "The America I Have Seen" he inveighed against American materialism, racism, individual freedom, its blatant sexuality and its lack of support for the Palestinian cause. Of women he wrote: "The American girl is well acquainted with her body's seductive capacity. She knows it lies in the face, and in expressive eyes, and thirsty lips. She knows seductiveness lies in the round breasts, the full buttocks, and in the shapely thighs, sleek legs—and she shows all this and does not hide it."

The American man's interest in violent sports disgusted him. He wrote: "This primitiveness can be seen in the spectacle of the fans as they follow a game of football…or watch boxing matches or bloody, monstrous wrestling matches… This spectacle leaves no room for doubt as to the primitiveness of the feelings of those who are enamored with muscular strength and desire it."

**Ramadan:** Originally a summer month in the pre-Islamic Arab calendar. The present Islamic calendar is lunar. Ramadan is the ninth month in the Islamic calendar. Its year is 11 to 12 days shorter than the solar year. As a result, Ramadan migrates throughout the seasons.

In 623 Mohammad led a force of caravan raiders to Badr where he intended to ambush a caravan headed for Mecca. The Quraysh of Mecca learned of his intentions and assembled a large army to defeat him and avenge the death of a fellow tribesman killed in an earlier caravan raid. Despite being significantly outnumbered, Mohammad's force overcame the Quraysh. This victory occurred early in the month of Ramadan and was regarded as a *furqan*, a sign of salvation. To commemorate the *furqan* Mohammad decreed that Muslims would fast during the month of Ramadan. It was first observed in 625.

During Ramadan Muslims who are able to fast during the daylight hours, neither eating nor drinking and abstaining from sexual intercourse and any vices. This fasting is one of the five pillars of Islam. The first three days of the next month are spent in celebrations, the Festival of Breaking Fast or *Eid ul-Fitr*.

Notes Arab-American educator Audrey Shabbas: "Ramadan is not only a month of 'moral abstinence.' It also has the social value of creating new bonds of understanding between all classes of people. The fast, practiced by the rich and poor alike, reminds the more fortunate members of society of the pangs of hunger which the poor suffer. Ramadan is especially a month of charity."

**Sharia law:** *Sharia* means "path to the water source" and refers to the body of Islamic religious law. *Sharia* forms the legal framework within which the public and some private aspects of life are regulated for those living in a legal system based on Muslim principles. *Sharia* deals with many aspects of day-to-day life, including politics, economics, banking, business, contracts, family, sexuality, hygiene, and social issues.

*Sharia* is less a strictly codified set of laws and more a system of devising laws, based on the *Quran*, *hadith*, consensus, analogy and centuries of interpretation, precedent and debate. Just as the *Quran* draws on non-Arabic sources, *sharia* shows traces of Bedouin law, commercial law from Mecca, agrarian law from Medina as well as Roman and Jewish law.

**Shia:** (See page 43)

**Succession:** It's generally agreed that the problem of succession to leadership in a body politic often places that body in a position of extreme vulnerability, particularly when there are rivals for power. This is what happened at the time of Mohammad's death. The Sunni/Shia split resulted.

After Mohammad's death the claimants included Abu Bakr, a longtime ally of Mohammad who was also the father of one of the Prophet's cherished wives, Aisha; Umar, an early Qurayshi foe of Mohammad who converted to Islam with a suddenness similar to Saul of Tarsus' conversion to become Paul, also the father of Mohammad's wife Hafsah; and Ali, a cousin and ward of Mohammad, husband of the Prophet's daughter Fatimah and father of his only surviving grandsons Hasan and Husayn. Abu Bakr was elected, but the Shia (Shiat Ali or partisans for Ali) resented the choice, contending that Mohammad had designated Ali, his cousin and son-in-law, as successor. For the sake of unity Ali agreed to Abu Bakr's election, but Mohammad's kinsmen were never happy with this result.

Abu Bakr served as *caliph* for two years (632-634) and was succeeded by Umar who organized and extended the Arab empire and served until 644 when he was fatally knifed by a Persian slave. Six electors again denied Ali as caliph and chose Uthman, a convert to Islam, member of an aristocratic Qurayshi clan and a former son-in-law of Mohammad. Uthman was murdered in 656. With the support of the distressed people of Medina Ali at last succeeded to the position of *caliph*. However, Aisha, now an influential widow of Mohammad, along with others from Mecca, accused Ali of complicity in Uthman's murder. She left Arabia in order to raise an army against him.

Contention between the two parties was launched. Any possibility of harmonizing matters with the Shia was lost when Ali's surviving son Husayn, along with most of the men of his family, was ambushed and assassinated near Karbala (now in Iraq) in 680. Today, there are still some tensions in certain arenas such as Iraq and Lebanon, but most Muslims coexist as simply that, Muslims.

**Suffism:** Sometimes called *Tassawuf* in Arabic is a mystical dimension within Islam that focuses on personal piety. Similar to Kabbalah mysticism in Judaism. A follower of Suffism is a Sufi. Derived from the word *Suf* which means wool, Suffis literally mean "wearer of wool," which in ancient times was associated with spirituality. Whirling dervishes, sometimes called Suffi spinning, are an attractive visible aspect within Suffism. Practitioners twirl for long periods of time in meditative focus only on God.

**Sunnah:** "the way of the prophet". The word *Sunnah* in Sunni Islam means those religious actions that were instituted by Mohammad during the 23 years of his ministry. Muslims initially received these through consensus of the companions of Mohammad and later through generation-to-generation transmission. Some Sunni regard the *sunnah* as those religious actions initiated by Abraham and later only revived by Mohammad.

**Sunni:** (See page 43)

**Tribalism:** Human beings' most basic—and most lasting—social structure, tribalism exists in many parts of the world. Tribes, formed of clans or lineages, are primarily based on blood- or kinship-ties, real or mythical. Even if these ties become highly attenuated, an ethnic or cultural bond remains strong. Often it is the sense of a common ancestor (e.g. the children of Israel). The smaller the group, the harsher the environment in which the tribe finds itself, the stronger the degree of loyalty that members feel to one another and the more group survival and community needs have primacy over individual needs. Tribes and clans are often egalitarian, without significant distinctions between members. Some primitive tribes have little tradition of individual ownership.

In the harsh environment of the Arabian steppes in the seventh century and before, life prospects were uncertain. Food was scarce and the competition for the necessities of life was intense. Since there was little chance that individuals or individual families could survive by themselves, nomads formed themselves into clans and tribes. Tribal membership demanded a rigorous and unquestioning loyalty to group and a commitment to defend—and avenge—other tribesmen. Individualism could not be accommodated. The ethic was egalitarian and goods and possessions were shared out equally. The tribal chief had responsibilities to take care of weaker members of the group. If tribesmen had obligations and codes to tribal brothers, these codes did not apply to members outside the tribe. The nomads' ethic was virile, masculine. Women were not highly regarded, but their reproductive power was prized: their bodies could produce other men. Since there was little in the way of material wealth, accumulating wives was a way of manifesting success and prestige.

As nomads adopted a settled life in villages, adherence to tribal obligations lessened. But the knowledge of tribal ties and connections remained. Even stronger were—and are—ties between family members. Here blood is certainly thicker than water.

**Umma:** When Mohammad and his followers left Mecca and emigrated to Medina, most Arabian societies were formed of tribes and clans held together by ties of blood and kinship. Medina was somewhat exceptional, an oasis inhabited by two previously nomadic Arab tribes as well as some Christian and some Jewish. Mohammed's emigrants represented a third Arab tribe along with a few non-Arabs.

Mohammad wished to convert Medina residents to Islam and so proclaimed an entirely new kind of "tribe," one based not on blood or kinship, but on religion: the *umma* or community of believers.

**Veiling women:** (See Hijab)

**Wahhabism:** (See page 40)

*—Thanks to Frederic Hunter for providing the "Glossary."*

# At a Glance
## Arab Countries - Important Muslim Countries

### Arab Countries
### Algeria
A North African country more than 3 times the size of Texas, Algeria has 44 million people, almost all of whom are Arab and/or Berber Sunni Muslims. Officially a socialist republic, the government does not encourage citizens to partic-

ipate in the political process. Opposing political parties are allowed, but parties based on religion or ethnic identity are outlawed. Relations with the US since 2001 have been warm, while those with France, which colonized the country, fluctuate. Algeria achieved independence in 1962. Its gas and oil reserves are the economy's mainstay, although they have done little to ameliorate the country's high unemployment.

## Bahrain

A small collection of islands in the Persian Gulf with a population of only 1.5 million, Bahrain is a constitutional monarchy dominated by its king. The November 2006 elections brought a Shiite majority to power in Parliament, but it is unclear whether King Hamad will allow the Parliament more than nominal legislative powers, and sectarian confrontations have increased since the elections. Bahrain's economy rests on its oil production and refining, although it is attempting to diversify into transport and services—particularly financial and media. Like most Gulf states, Bahrain has warm relations with the United States and Europe, and in July 2008 sent its first Jewish female ambassador to the United States.

## Comoros

The Comoros is a small grouping of islands off southern Africa with just under 700,000 people, almost all Sunni Muslim. The country is a republic based on the confederated union of the islands, with the presidency rotating every four years to the elected president of one of the Comoros' three main islands and a unicameral legislature. The country is extremely poor, with a weak economy that depends heavily on agriculture and remittances from citizens working abroad.

## Djibouti

A small African country on the mouth of the Red Sea, Djibouti has 1.1 million people, the majority Somali and Afar, and the vast majority of whom are Sunni Muslim. Djibouti is a republic with a president and a unicameral chamber of deputies. The governing party currently holds all seats. The country's economy is heavily service-based, relating to its position at the intersection of the Red Sea and the Gulf of Aden. It has little in the way of natural resources and few exports. The country enjoys warm relations with France and the United States, which has opened a military base there.

## Egypt

One of the larger countries of the Arab world, Egypt has 109 million people, mostly Muslim with a Coptic Christian minority. The "Arab Spring" protests for democracy toppled "president for life" Mubarak and after some tense growing pains has a stable system compared to some of its neighbors. Religious and ethnic political parties are banned, and since 2001 the government has been increasingly intolerant of any expression of opposition. Nonetheless, the Muslim Brotherhood remains the state's most powerful opposition group, and civil society groups remain active. Egypt's economy is privatizing, and exports are growing, but for the average Egyptian the economic picture remains bleak. While European countries have pressured Egypt to respect human rights laws and accelerate reforms, the United States views the country as a strong ally in anti-terror initiatives and treats it warmly.

## Iraq

A medium-large country in the heart of the Arab world, Iraq has roughly 43 million people, who are mostly Arab, with a sizeable Kurdish and smaller Turkoman and Assyrian minorities. They are almost all Muslim, with Shi'a approaching two-thirds of the population. Iraq is technically a democracy, although the deep instability there makes the elected government's capacity for governance questionable. Religious parties are actively involved in politics although they tend to join with other parties when contesting elections. Today Iraq's economy depends on oil revenues and aid from the United States government. Relations with other countries in and beyond the region are greatly conditioned by the ongoing US occupation.

## Jordan

Jordan is a medium-small, land-locked country, with a population of just under 11 million, most of whom are Sunni Muslim and many of Palestinian origin. Relations between Jordan's Palestinian and Bedouin populations, and between Jordan and Israel, have dominated the country's political realm, which is a king-dominated constitutional monarchy with an appointed cabinet and a weak bicameral assembly. Political parties are allowed, although the strongest opposition movement is the Muslim Brotherhood, which has a separate political party. The economy is weak. Jordan has few natural resources and has struggled with efforts to develop private and semi-private industry. Jordan is a major United States aid recipient and has enjoyed particularly warm relations with the US since the outbreak of the second Gulf war in 1990.

## Kuwait

A small Gulf state made famous by the 1990 Iraqi invasion, Kuwait's 2.5 million people are a mixture of Kuwaiti, Arab, and Asian ethnicities. Roughly four in five are Muslim, of whom three in 10 are Shi'a. The rest are Christian or other religions—with most of these foreign workers rather than citizens. The country is a constitutional emirate, with a unicameral assembly whose capacity for meaningful governing activity has varied over time. Kuwait's economy is heavily dependent on its oil exports. The country has few natural resources and limited industry. Kuwait's relations with European states and the United States are warm. It hosts the United States' major military base and Iraq staging area.

## Lebanon

A small Levantine state on the coast of the Mediterranean, Lebanon's nearly 5.5 million people are a mix of ethnicities and religions, the vast majority Arab and six in ten Muslim. A titular republic, Lebanon's complicated political system dictates the religion of the president, prime minister, and speaker of parliament, with the unicameral parliament's seats also allocated by religion. Political "parties" tend to be short-lived groupings around individual leaders rather than sustained institutions. Lebanon's economy is increasingly service and remittance based, with a growing tourist sector—although the viability of any sector is in question after the 2006 war between Israel and the Lebanon-based Hezbollah and the political infighting since then. Lebanon enjoys warm relations with European states and the United States, with France and the United States each aligning behind particular figures and political movements.

## Libya

One of the largest Arab world countries, Libya's 7 million people are located in the middle of North Africa. Almost entirely Arab and/or Berber Sunni Muslims, Libyans live in an idiosyncratic socialist republic created by Revolutionary Leader-for-life Mu'ammar al-Qadhafi nearly forty years ago. Qadhafi was overthrown and killed as part of the Arab Spring revolt for freedom. The country has fallen into disarray with varied powerbrokers and tribal elements controlling different parts of the country.

## Mauritania

A medium-large country in northwest Africa, Mauritania has nearly 4.6 million people, all Muslim and evenly distributed among mixed Arab/Berber and African ethnicities. Although technically a republic, Mauritania is currently under the control of a military council, and opposition and Islamist parties are banned. The country's economy is heavily agriculture based, although its rich iron deposits comprise its largest export category. Mauritania's long-standing economic woes are expected to be offset by its entry into oil production, although this has been delayed by the country's political instability. While not particularly close to the United States, Mauritania has successfully cultivated good relations with Spain and other European states.

## Morocco

The westernmost country in the Arab world, Morocco also has one of the largest populations: 33 million people, almost all Arab and/or Berber Muslims. The government is a king-dominated constitutional monarchy with a weak bicameral parliament. Although Morocco has well-known Islamists, the primary organized opposition comes from workers' groups. While agriculture, industry and services all share similar percentages of the country's GDP, the economy itself is weak, and many people suffer from poverty and unemployment. Morocco has seen its global image improve drastically due to great successes in international sports after it became the first Arab or African nation to make it to the World Cup semifinals and finished fourth overall. Morocco enjoys warm relations with the United States as well as France and other European states.

## Oman

Another small Gulf state, Oman's 4.5 million citizens are a mix of Arab, Indian, and South Asian ethnicities, three-quarters of whom are Ibadhi Muslim and the rest Sunni, Shi'a, and some minority religions. The country is under a strong monarchy, with a bicameral parliament that plays only a consulting role. While the current economy is supported by oil and gas production, the government has made substantive commitments to liberalization, training and hiring initiatives to strengthen the Omani workforce and develop local industry. Oman's moderate politics have enabled it to enjoy cordial relations with its neighbors as well as other countries.

## Palestine

A territory that currently enjoys a degree of self-governance under severe military, political and economic restrictions, Palestine today is technically not a country but rather a zone under Israeli military control. Its land is split into two non-contiguous blocks, with the Palestinian Authority currently controlling Palestine's land in the West Bank and Hamas governing the Gaza Strip. There are approximately 2.4 million Palestinians in the West Bank, and 1.5 in the Gaza Strip. The total Palestinian population worldwide is estimated to be between 10 and 11 million people, over half of whom are stateless refugees with no legal citizenship in any country. The vast majority of Palestinians are Sunni Muslims, although there is a significant Christian minority as well as several smaller religious communities.

## Qatar

One of the Gulf's smaller states, Qatar perches at the tip of Saudi Arabia. Its 2.6 million inhabitants include roughly 450,000 resident workers, most from India, Pakistan, and the Philippines, who have residency but not citizenship. Approximately nine in ten Qataris are Sunni Muslims and follow the conservative Wahhabi interpretation found in Saudi Arabia, while the rest are Shi'a. The country is an emirate, with a consultative council for which elections were last held in 1970. Qatar's economic strength rests upon its oil and gas production, of which it has the world's third largest reserve. Qatar enjoys good relations with European states and close relations with the United States, which has two military bases there. Al Jazeera, the well-known Arabic satellite television network, is based in Qatar. Qatar hosted the World Cup in 2022 and gained international acclaim for its execution.

## Saudi Arabia

This massive country physically dominates the Gulf, although its harsh climate supports a population of only 36 million, of whom nearly 5.6 million are foreign workers. Saudis are mostly Sunni and largely Arab, with small Shi'a and African/Asian ethnic and religious minorities, many of whom have faced discrimination. The government is a strong monarchy, with a consultative council whose members are appointed rather than elected. The Saud family dominates the top echelons of government, occupying the major ministry, cabinet, and diplomatic posts. This effectively curtails private political activity. The government's primary opposition comes from Islamist groups. Saudi Arabia's economy is heavily dependent upon revenues from its massive oil reserves, although it has made efforts to develop related industries. The country enjoys warm relations with the United States despite the latter's 2003 military withdrawal, caused by popular protests within the Kingdom.

## Somalia

A medium-large country in Eastern Africa, Somalia's roughly 17 million people are Sunni Muslim, with more than four in five Somali and the rest Bantu and other ethnicities. The country has suffered from internal disorder for years and is currently under the control of a disputed transnational government. The economy is divided among several autonomous regions, and generally dependent upon agriculture and livestock exports, as well as remittances from those able to work abroad. Somalia and/or its sub-divisions do not have substantial relations with the United States. Most state relations in recent years have related to efforts to stabilize the country, which have been primarily led by the United Nations and Kenya, or to economic activity, in which the United Arab Emirates and Saudi Arabia, whose ban on Somali beef exports has had a noticeable economic impact, have played the largest roles.

## Sudan

Africa's largest nation, Sudan has over 49 million people, the majority African, nearly 70% Arab and the rest a mixture. Seven in 10 are Sunni Muslim, with most of the rest animist and a small minority Christian. The country is currently under a two-party national unity government, although great instability remains throughout much of Sudan. Political parties are allowed, but they have limited ability to exert any degree of power in a country where the rule of law is so contested. The economy is stronger than the country's long civil war would suggest, thanks to oil exports, but deep poverty remains. Relations with Europe and the United States are primarily linked to aid, crisis intervention (especially related to the western region of Darfur), and anti-terrorism initiatives.

## South Sudan

After a referendum in 2011, what was formerly the southern third of Sudan, seceded and became its own country called South Sudan. It has a population of approximately 11 million inhabitants, approximately 60% Christian, 32% folk religion, and approximately 6% Muslim. While Arabic is spoken there, English is the official language and the people are overwhelmingly not Arab, rather a range of local ethnic groups such as Dinka and Nuer.

## Syria

A medium-sized country in the heart of the Middle East, Syria has nearly 19 million people, mostly Arab but with measurable Kurdish and Armenian populations. Nearly three in four are Sunni Muslims, with minority Muslim sects, Christians, and a sprinkling of Jews comprising the remainder. Technically a republic, Syria is governed as a one-party state under a socialist but authoritarian regime led by the Baath Party. Certain political parties are approved, although parties with ethnic or religious identities and those that do not meet Ba'ath Party approval are not. Opposition comes from several outside organizations as well as Kurdish, Islamist, and democratic groups inside Syria. The country's economy depends greatly on its oil revenues, but in the face of the imminent depletion of its oil reserves, the government has begun accelerating economic reforms. These reforms often have proven more unpopular with local private enterprise than government officials, and reduction of government subsidies on basic commodities has forced the largely lower- and middle-class population to confront inflation and a rising cost of living. The country continues to reel from a costly civil war that has consumed it, destroyed culture, history, and the will of the people and helped birth what became ISIS/DAESH. Instability and uncertainty continue as the new normal.

### Tunisia

A medium small North African country, Tunisia has just over 12 million people, almost all Arab and Muslim. Tunisia is the spark that ignited what came to be known as the Arab Spring. On December 17, 2010, a street vendor named Mohamed Bouazizi set himself aflame in front of the governor's office. He did so as a response to constant police abuse and extortion. He is said to have exclaimed "How am I supposed to make a living" before lighting himself on fire. Within hours protests began percolating, and it became the catalyst for the sweeping pro-democracy movement across the Arab world, known as the Arab Spring. Unfortunately, while regime change did take place, Tunisia is far from a blossoming democracy, but has potential. It has also gained some international respect through tennis sensation Ons Jabeur, ranked number 2 in the world at one point and the highest ranked Arab or Muslim tennis player in history.

### United Arab Emirates (UAE)

Another small Gulf state, the United Arab Emirates' seven emirates have 9 million inhabitants, of whom perhaps 500,000 are Emirati. Arabs, Iranians, and South Asians make up the bulk of the population. The overwhelming majority of the population is Muslim, with a measurable Shi'a presence, and a very small Christian and Hindu minority. The Emirates are a federation, with the president chosen from Abu Dhabi and the prime minister/vice president from Dubai. There is a unicameral consultative council made up of members appointed by each emirate, but Dubai and Abu Dhabi dominate. The Emirati economy depends heavily on its oil and gas exports, which keep the country's GDP high. Real estate investments and developments in financial and other services are notable in Dubai and Abu Dhabi. The UAE enjoys warm relations with Europe and the United States, despite the failed 2006 Dubai Ports deal. Dubai and Abu

Dhabi have shone as international cities with glamour, fame, and affluence with a strong international attraction.

## Yemen

A medium-large state on the southern side of the Gulf, Yemen has nearly 34 million people, most of whom are Arab, with African-Arab and South Asian mixes. The population is largely Muslim, with measurable Muslim minority Shafi'i and Zaydi communities, as well as small Christian, Jewish, and Hindu populations. A republic was established after the 1990 unification of north and south; the president has also been in power since then. In 2014, a civil war broke out once again and has become a proxy war between Saudi Arabia and Iran, with varying factors and a growing humanitarian crisis. The economy is very poor, and the people are suffering.

## Important Countries and Regions in the Larger Muslim World
### Afghanistan

A large, landlocked country located approximately at the center of Asia, Afghanistan has served as a natural crossroads between the East and the West and an ancient focal point of trade and migration. With a population estimated at 40 million, overwhelmingly Muslim but ethnically mixed, it has religious, ethno-linguistic, and geographic links with its neighbors: Pakistan in the south and east, Iran in the west, Turkmenistan, Uzbekistan and Tajikistan in the north, and China in the far northeast. During its long history, the land has seen various invaders and conquerors. Since the late 1970s Afghanistan has suffered continuous and brutal civil war, as well as invasions from the Soviets in 1979 and from the 2001 US-led coalition following Al-Qaeda's September 2001 attacks.

The Taliban government, which took control following the Soviet withdrawal, permitted Al-Qaeda training camps on its territory. The US-led invasion toppled this government. In late 2001 the United Nations Security Council authorized the creation of an International Security Assistance Force, composed of NATO troops that were involved in assisting the government of President Hamid Karzai. In 2005 the United States and Afghanistan signed a strategic partnership agreement committing both nations to a long-term relationship. In the meantime, billions of dollars have also been provided by the international community as aid for the reconstruction of the country. Despite gains against the Taliban and Al-Qaeda, the Taliban remains a presence in the country. Based now in mountainous, tribal areas of northwest Pakistan, it has regained strength and represents a significant military challenge to the Karzai government and its allies. In August 2021, the US withdrew its troops from Afghanistan and the Taliban took control once more bringing their draconian methods to rule. Violent extremist groups such have also capitalized on the chaos.

## Bangladesh

A country in South Asia, Bangladesh was established by the partition of Bengal and India in 1947, when the region became the eastern wing of the newly-formed Pakistan. However, a distance of 1000 miles separated this eastern wing from Pakistan's larger, western wing. Although both have majority-Muslim populations, large ethnic differences separated the two halves of Pakistan. Political and linguistic discrimination as well as economic neglect led to popular agitations against West Pakistan, culminating in the war for independence in 1971 and the establishment of Bangladesh. Among the most densely populated countries in the world, with a population of 172 million, Bangladesh has endured famines, cyclones, tsunamis, monsoon floods and widespread poverty, as well as political turmoil and several military coups. The government is a parliamentary democracy. However, political rule has been suspended under the emergency law imposed in January 2007. According to the World Bank's July 2005 Country Brief, the country has made significant progress in human development in the areas of literacy, gender parity in schooling and reduction of population growth—but it continues to face significant challenges.

## Indonesia

Indonesia, located in Southeast Asia, is composed of 17,508 islands. With a population of over 270 million, it is the world's fourth most populous country and the most populous Muslim-majority nation. Officially, it is not an Islamic state, but a republic, with an elected parliament and president. Following three and a half centuries of Dutch colonial rule, Indonesia secured its independence after World War II. Its history has since been turbulent, with challenges posed by natural disasters, corruption, separatism, a democratization process, and periods of rapid economic change. The country has been held together, nonetheless, by a shared identity defined by a national language, a majority-Muslim population, and a history of colonialism and anti-colonial opposition. However, sectarian tensions and separatism have led to violent confrontations that have undermined political and economic stability. Despite its large population and densely populated regions, Indonesia has vast areas of wilderness which give it the world's second highest level of biodiversity.

**Iran**

The world's 18th-largest country in terms of surface area, Iran is located in Central Eurasia and stretches to the northeastern shore of the Persian Gulf. Historically known as Persia, Iran has a population of over 90 million, which is Aryan or Persian, with small Arab, Armenian and Azeri Turkish minorities. Home to one of the world's oldest continuous major civilizations, with historical and urban settlements dating back to 4000 BC, Iran today occupies an important position in international energy security and the world economy because of its large reserves of petroleum and natural gas. After centuries of foreign occupation and short-lived native dynasties, Iran was reunified as an independent state in 1501 by a dynasty promoting Shi'a Islam as the official religion. This marked one of the most important turning points in the history of Islam, as Iran is the only Muslim country with a majority-Shi'a population.

For most of its history, Iran's government was a monarchy ruled by a shah. The Pahlavis came to power in the early 1900s as military leaders with no royal blood, but they adopted the title shah as well. The Iranian revolution marked the country's transformation into an Islamic republic, which happened officially on April 1, 1979.

Iran's political system comprises several intricately connected governing bodies. The Supreme Leader of Iran, Ayatollah Ali Khamenei, is responsible for delineation and supervision of the general policies of the Islamic Republic. Next in line is the current president, Mahmoud Ahmadinejad, elected in 2005 for a four-year term.

The United States' relationship with Iran has been strained since the Islamic revolution, due partly to a series of pre-Revolution events. In 1951 Dr. Mohammed Mossadegh was elected Iran's prime minister and became enormously popular by nationalizing Iran's oil reserves. In retaliation Britain embargoed Iranian oil and sought American help in overthrowing Mossadegh. This was provided by President Dwight D. Eisenhower. Mossadegh was deposed and arrested. With American support Shah Mohammad Reza Pahlavi rapidly modernized Iranian infrastructure, but simultaneously crushed all forms of political opposition with his intelligence agency, SAVAK.

Ayatollah Ruhollah Khomeini became an active critic of the shah, publicly denounced the government, and was sent into exile. His return to Iran in the late 1970s triggered the Iranian Revolution, a popular movement that overthrew the Shah and brought Khomeini to power. Part of this revolutionary fervor was directed against the United States, which gave refuge to the deposed shah and his family. In November 1979 Iranian students seized US embassy personnel and held 52 of them hostage for more than 14 months.

Iraqi leader Saddam Hussein decided to take advantage of what he perceived to be disorder in the wake of the Iranian Revolution and its unpopularity with Western governments. In September 1980 the Iraqi army invaded Iran at Khuzestan, a region with a substantial Arab population as well as rich oil fields. Although Saddam Hussein's army made early advances, Iranian forces managed to push it back into Iraq. Khomeini sought to export his Islamic revolution westward into Iraq, especially on the majority Shi'a Arabs. The war continued until 1988, when Khomeini, in his words, "drank the cup of poison" and accepted a truce mediated by the United Nations. The total Iranian casualties of the war were estimated to be between 500,000 and 1,000,000. Almost all relevant international agencies have confirmed that Saddam engaged in chemical warfare to blunt Iranian human wave attacks.

Today, Iran is developing nuclear capabilities for domestic energy consumption, a move that has alarmed the United States and many members of the international community. Tensions between the two countries remain.

### Malaysia

A country in Southeast Asia with a population of over 34 million, Malaysia consists of two regions, Peninsular Malaysia and Malaysian Borneo, separated by the South China Sea. Today comprising 13 states and three federal territories, Malaysia did not exist as a unified state until 1963. At that time several former British-ruled territories on the Malay Peninsula, which had been independent since 1957, joined forces with the territories of Sabah and Sarawak on the northern coast of Borneo.

Malaysia is a constitutional monarchy, nominally headed by a paramount ruler and a bicameral Parliament consisting of a non-elected upper house and an elected lower house. All Peninsular Malaysian states have hereditary rulers except those of Melaka and Penang. Those two states, along with Sabah and Sarawak, have governors appointed by the government.

Malaysia is an ethnically mixed country, with Malays forming the majority of the population. There are also sizable Chinese and Indian communities, as well as a small minority of Arab descent. Islam is both the largest and the official religion. With Malaysia being one of the three countries controlling the strategic Strait of Malacca, international trade plays a large role in the country's economy.

### Pakistan

A country in South Asia with a population of 241 million, Pakistan is the world's sixth most populous country and has the world's second-largest Muslim population after Indonesia. It is located in the home of one of the world's oldest civilizations, that of the Indus Valley, where civilized life dates back at least 5,000 years. The area has seen invasions from the Persians, Greeks, Scythians, Arabs, Afghans, and Turks. The British later dominated the region.

The separation in 1947 of British India into the Muslim state of Pakistan (with West and East sections) and largely Hindu India was never satisfactorily resolved, and India and Pakistan fought two wars (in 1947-48 and 1965) over the disputed Kashmir territory. A third war in 1971, in which India capitalized on the marginalization of Bengalis in Pakistani politics by fostering opposition to Islamabad's rule, resulted in East Pakistan becoming the separate nation of Bangladesh. In response to Indian nuclear weapons testing, Pakistan conducted its own tests in 1998. The dispute over the state of Kashmir is ongoing, but discussions and confidence-building measures have led to decreased tensions since 2002.

While officially an Islamic Republic with scheduled elections for Parliament and the presidency, an October 1999 military coup brought to power General Pervez Musharraf who named himself president in June, 2001. Following the 9/11 attacks Musharraf made Pakistan a crucial ally in the US war on terror despite considerable internal sympathy for Afghanistan's Taliban government. Musharraf's serving as both president and head of the army caused challenges from the Supreme Court, but he managed to be re-elected president in November 2007 by reconstituting the court and resigning his military post. The strains between Musharraf and his supporters and the ousted Supreme Court justices and theirs, in addition to Musharraf's support of the US war on terror, have caused concern in Washington about Pakistan's internal stability. After a return to civilian government in early-2008, Musharraf faced the likelihood of impeachment and in August resigned the presidency. Shortly afterwards the coalition governing the country fractured seeming to justify fears of the country's political instability. In addition, a resurgent Taliban has used Pakistan's northwestern frontier areas, over which the central government has limited control, to launch renewed attacks into Afghanistan.

### Turkey

A Eurasian country stretching across the Anatolian peninsula in western Asia into the Balkan region of southeastern Europe, Turkey's strategic location astride two continents has given its culture a unique blend of Eastern and Western tradition. A powerful regional presence in the Eurasian landmass with strong historic, cultural and economic influence in the area between the European Union in the west and Central Asia in the east, Russia in the north and the Middle East in the south, Turkey possesses considerable strategic significance. With some 84 million inhabitants, it is a democratic, secular, unitary, constitutional republic whose political system was established in 1923 under the leadership of Mustafa Kemal Atatürk, following the fall of the Ottoman Empire in the aftermath of World War I. Atatürk set the country on a strongly secular course, introducing wide-ranging social, legal, and political reforms.

After a period of one-party rule, the 1950 election victory of the opposition Democratic Party led to a peaceful transfer of power. Turkish democracy has been interrupted by intermittent military coups (1960, 1971, 1980, 2016), which in each case eventually resulted in a return of political power to civilians. In 1997, the military helped engineer the ouster of the then Islamic-oriented government. Questions about the military's intentions of enforcing the country's secular orientation arose in mid-2007 when the present government led by the Islamic-leaning Justice and Development Party of Prime Minister Recep Tayyip Erdogan sought to elect its candidate Abdullaah Gul as president and succeeded in doing so without military intervention.

Turkey is a member of NATO and is currently seeking membership in the European Union, which was halted as late as 2019, but the issue continues to be raised. A separatist insurgency begun in 1984 by the Kurdistan Workers' Party (PKK) has dominated the military's attention, claiming more than 30,000 lives. After the capture of the group's leader in 1999, the insurgents largely withdrew to northern Iraq. To resist incursions from this area, Turkey sent troops into northern Iraq in the spring of 2008. It has played an integral role in serving as a mediator in international conflicts from Ukraine/Russia to Israel/Palestine.

### "Kurdistan"

Not a country at all, but rather the dream of a country cherished by the Kurdish people who hoped that the end of the Ottoman Empire would give them a nation-state. Kurds live on an extensive plateau and mountainous area in the Middle East. It covers large parts of eastern Turkey, northern Iraq, northwestern Iran and smaller parts of northern Syria and Armenia. The national aspirations of the Kurds (estimated population: 25 to 30 million) have complicated the politics of those countries with large Kurdish populations.

The Kurds of northern Iraq have created a region which has gained official recognition internationally as an autonomous federal entity.

Today the majority of Kurds are Muslim, although their interpretation of

Muslim faith and practice frequently differs from Arab and other forms. Their faith tends to be less assertive than that of Muslims in other areas. For example, Kurdish women do not cover their faces, their hijab is less restrictive, and they do not wear full-cover garments such as the Iranian chador or Arabic abaya.

### The Sahel Region of Africa

The Sahel is a semi-arid tropical savanna ecoregion in Africa, which forms the transition between the Sahara desert to the north and the more fertile region to the south. It runs 2,400 miles from the Atlantic Ocean in the west to the Red Sea in the east, in a belt that varies from several hundred to a thousand kilometers in width. The countries of the Sahel include Senegal, Mauritania, Mali, Burkina Faso, Niger, Nigeria, Chad, and Sudan. Over the history of Africa the region has been home to some of the most advanced kingdoms benefiting from trade across the desert. Muslim traders brought Islam to the region. Significant portions of the population are now Muslim.

### From the Caucasus across the Steppes of Central Asia

Muslim populations inhabit the vast area that lies between the Caucasus mountains and the Uighur areas of western China. In ancient times the Great Steppe of Central Asia, a valuable prize for invaders, including Attila the Hun, Genghis Khan and Tamerlane, was crossed by the Silk Road, the trade route that linked western Europe to China. Following the implosion of the Soviet Union, nation-states were created in this area: Kazakhstan, Turkmenistan. Uzbekistan, Kyrgystan, Tajikistan. They seem remote to us, but comprise a part of the Muslim World.

### The Muslim Diaspora

In recent years the world has witnessed large migrations of people from the less developed parts of the world to those developed parts which offer the hope of jobs, education and higher standards of living. Large groups of Muslims have been part of these migrations: Pakistanis to England; Turks to Germany; Tunisians, Algerians, and Moroccans to France; Moroccans to Spain and the Netherlands. Earlier migrations in particular brought Syrians to the United States and Lebanese throughout the world. Accommodating these immigrants has severely challenged the receiving societies, especially when Muslim immigrants wished to take advantage of jobs and welfare benefits without any desire to change their lifeways. Dashed expectations, bitterness at the injustices and humiliation of prejudice and cultural misunderstanding have produced fertile ground for recruiting disaffected young Muslims as terrorists. Fortunately, most Arab and Muslim immigrants to the United States have been able to integrate into the larger population, enjoying relatively high standards of living relative to the population as a whole. As a result they have tended to minimize acts of racism and discrimination, not wanting to jeopardize their security by criticizing their adopted country.

*—Thanks to Andrea Stanton for providing "At a Glance."*

# Acknowledgements

THE AUTHOR WISHES TO EXTEND HIS MOST HEARTFELT gratitude to all the good souls that came together to make this book a reality. Perhaps most notably, the man behind Cune Press, Scott Davis. In 2006, I was a fairly unknown author (a poetry book and a few small publications) and had hired a grad student to send out manuscripts for almost a year. It was a vicious cycle; publishers didn't want me because I didn't have an agent; agents didn't want me because I hadn't been published. At a time when no one was willing to take a chance on a book based on my seminars, Scott did not hesitate. In late 2020, Scott reached out to me once again. He believed it was time for a third edition. His research suggested changing the name and we secured wonderful new endorsements and I revised and updated with all my heart what would be known as "Muslims, Arabs, and Arab-Americans." One of the last communications with Scott was him letting me know he agreed with my new cover suggestion and that it would now be its own stand-alone book. That happy euphoria is literally the last memory I have of this wonderful man. Rest in Power and Peace Scott, thank you for everything. I would be remiss, if I did not mention the remainder of the team, from Mary Davis – who took over the helm at Cune Press; to the incredibly patient and kind Brenda Pierce; to the soft edits and wisdom of Steven Schlesser and Frederic Hunter's prior edits and support; Ali Farzat and Mamoun Sakkal's unmatched talents.

In a time of constant societal tests, I am humbled by those who were willing to endorse me and this book, Daveed Gartenstein-Ross, Kristina Tanasichuk, Rabbi Victor Urecki, Brie Loskota, and Maz Jobrani. Thank you from the bottom of my heart.

Finally, I want to express my most sincere love for my parents, Waseem and Zayada Shora, who had the wisdom to immigrate to my America and deposit my brother and I, as an investment to this great nation. To mom, I am the soul I am today, because of you and the love, compassion, and optimism you taught me. To my one and only son, Jawad, you are the greatest gift I lay upon the feet of the world, may you grow to be as great as your greatest ancestors. Last, but not least, my partner, my soundboard, my greatest adventure, my love, my You, my Hala… thank you for letting me love you the way you always deserved.

This book is dedicated to my grandparents – who are long gone – and my grandchildren – who are not even a twinkle in the eye yet. This book is meant to honor my past ancestors and future generations. I hope it makes some dent of a positive impact on the world.

# The Calligraphy of Mamoun Sakkal

**M**AMOUN SAKKAL, CALLIGRAPHY ARTIST (background calligraphy; section pages) of this book, is a leading Arabic calligrapher who has won international competitions for his calligraphic and typographic work. Sakkal has designed typefaces that adapt Arabic to the requirements of computer text and modern commerce. His creations include a computer typeface for Uighur, the Turkic-derived tongue of a Muslim minority in remote Western China. Sakkal has adapted Kufic (an angular Arabic script) as a decorative element for architectural design and even as a building form. The following samples are from Sakkal's work-in-progress: *The Principles of Square Kufic Design*. For more: www. sakkaldesign.com.

# The Political Cartoons of Ali Farzat

ALI FARZAT, THE ILLUSTRATOR OF THIS BOOK, is the leading Arab political cartoonist. He serves as head of the Arab Cartoonists' Association and publishes widely in Arab and European publications. The BBC is currently developing animations based on Farzat caricatures. Characteristically, Farzat cartoons appear without captions. The following caricatures are from Farzat's book: *A Pen of Damascus Steel: The Political Cartoons of an Arab Master*. For more: www.alifarzat.com.

# Index

# About Cune Press

CUNE PRESS WAS FOUNDED IN 1994 TO PUBLISH thoughtful writing of public importance. Our name is derived from "cuneiform." (In Latin *cuni* means "wedge.")

In the ancient Near East the development of cuneiform script—simpler and more adaptable than hieroglyphics—enabled a large class of merchants and landowners to become literate. Clay tablets inscribed with wedge-shaped stylus marks made possible a broad inter-meshing of individual efforts in trade and commerce.

Cuneiform enabled scholarship to exist and art to flower, and created what historians define as the world's first civilization. When the Phoenicians developed their sound-based alphabet, they expressed it in cuneiform.

The idea of Cune Press is the democratization of learning, the faith that rarefied ideas, pulled from dusty pedestals and displayed in the streets, can transform the lives of ordinary people. And it is the conviction that ordinary people, trusted with the most precious gifts of civilization, will give our culture elasticity and depth—a necessity if we are to survive in a time of rapid change.

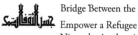 Aswat: Voices from a Small Planet (a series from Cune Press)

| | |
|---|---|
| Looking Both Ways | Pauline Kaldas |
| Stage Warriors | Sarah Imes Borden |
| Stories My Father Told Me | Helen Zughaib & Elia Zughaib |
| Girl Fighters | Carolyn Han |

Syria Crossroads (a series from Cune Press)

| | |
|---|---|
| Leaving Syria | Bill Dienst & Madi Williamson |
| Explore the Old City of Aleppo | Khaldoun Fansa |
| Steel & Silk | Sami Moubayed |
| The Dusk Visitor | Musa Al-Halool |
| The Road from Damascus | Scott C. Davis |
| A Pen of Damascus Steel | Ali Ferzat |
| White Carnations | Musa Rahum Abbas |

Bridge Between the Cultures (a series from Cune Press)

| | |
|---|---|
| Empower a Refugee | Patricia Martin Holt |
| Nietzsche Awakens! | Farid Younes |
| Afghanistan & Beyond | Linda Sartor |
| Apartheid Is a Crime | Mats Svensson |
| Finding Melody Sullivan | Alice Rothchild |
| Confessions of a Knight Errant | Gretchen McCullough |
| Sand Paper Stone | Duncan Lyon |

 Cune   Cune Press: www.cunepress.com

# About the Author

**N**AWAR SHORA HAS SPENT HIS TWO-DECADE PLUS CAREER at the intersection of civil rights/DEIA and national security/counterterrorism with expertise and accolades across the spectrum.

The positive impact of his groundbreaking outreach efforts in the immediate aftermath of the 9/11 attacks remain through today. He is a nationally recognized authority and subject matter expert on community outreach and stakeholder engagement as well as cultural demystification and Diversity, Equity, Inclusion and Access (DEIA) efforts.

Nawar has delivered in-person trainings to more than 100,000 professionals, including intelligence analysts, law enforcement officers, university professors and students, houses of worship, and corporate security and executive groups. He approaches intimidating and difficult topics with humor, diplomacy and charm. He has been called the "Arab Robin Williams" by members of the NYPD and is often compared to the late comedian for his high energy, wit, and occasional Freudian joke.

Nawar's experience ranges between intimate one-on-one advisory sessions with the upper echelon of the US government to public keynotes before 14,000 individuals. In 2018, he testified as a witness to the U.S. Senate Committee on Homeland Security and Governmental Affairs. That year, he was also invited back to his Alma Matter, Marshall University, to keynote the commencement ceremony with a theme of "Conquer your reality". He has served as a guest lecturer at varied academic institutions, UPS's Security Information Group, the Federal Law Enforcement Training Center (FLETC), the FBI Academy, National Counterterrorism Center, Terrorist Screening Center, and countless other private and public institutions. He has provided insights to the most inner depths of the US

Government and has worked with most of the three letter agencies except the NSA, but figured they must be listening in anyway!

Nawar's efforts have been recognized by the FBI with the Director's Community Leadership Award, the DHS Outstanding American by Choice Award, the FBI Exceptional Service in the Public Interest Award, the Department of Homeland Security's Office for Civil Rights and Civil Liberties Leadership Award, the Washington, DC Metro Police Department's Outstanding and Dedicated Service Award, FBI Community Outreach Training Award, among many more.

Nawar is a highly sought-after public speaker, connector, and bridge-builder. He discusses the history, norms, mores, culture, and current events of the Arab and Muslim worlds with an eye towards amplifying our humanity and the fabric of our American values. His stories on failure, grace, and inspiration make him a unique motivational presence.